TOP 10
MADEIRA

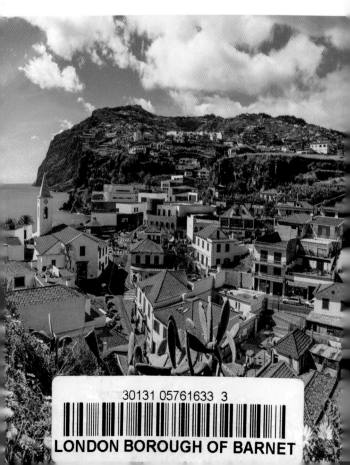

Top 10 Madeira Highlights

The Top 10 of Everything

CONTENTS

Madeira
Area by Area

Streetsmart

Within each Top 10 list in this book, no hierarchy of quality or popularity is implied. All 10 are, in the editor's opinion, of roughly equal merit.

Title page, front cover and spine *The picturesque Câmara de Lobos village, Madeira*
Back cover, clockwise fom top left *The altar at Igreja Matriz, São Vicente; terrace of a restaurant overlooking the sailing port in Madeira; tourists at the seafront promenade in Funchal; Câmara de Lobos; panoramic view from Cabo Girão, Madeira's highest cliff*

The rapid rate at which the world is changing is constantly keeping the DK Eyewitness team on our toes. While we've worked hard to ensure that this edition of Madeira is accurate and up-to-date, we know that opening hours alter, standards shift, prices fluctuate, places close and new ones pop up in their stead. So, if you notice we've got something wrong or left something out, we want to hear about it. Please get in touch at **travelguides@dk.com**

Welcome to
Madeira

With its sun-soaked beaches, beautiful parks and hills etched with an extraordinary network of *levada* footpaths, Madeira is a scenic masterpiece. This subtropical island is also a culturally rich destination that is steeped in tradition and celebrated for its world-class wine. With DK Eyewitness Top 10 Madeira, it is yours to explore.

Madeira's lively capital Funchal is built around centuries of history: its lovely **cathedral** dates from the 16th century and there are fabulous Flemish artworks in the **Museu de Arte Sacra**. Linger in **Museu da Quinta das Cruzes**, the home of João Gonçalves Zarco, who claimed Madeira for Portugal in 1419. Wander the **Zona Velha** (Old Town), now full of vibrant bars, hip galleries and enviable eateries.

Away from the city, Madeira is a popular outdoors destination. The walking and hiking is among the best in Europe, with some trails crowning the island's highest peaks and others snaking through the UNESCO-listed ***laurissilva* forest**. Warm, crystal blue waters offer opportunity for watersports and truly memorable whale- and dolphin-watching trips. Neighbouring **Porto Santo** is worth a detour, not least for its magnificent golden sandy beaches.

Whether you're visiting for a weekend or a week, our Top 10 guide brings together the best of everything Madeira has to offer, from historic buildings and churches to wine outlets and specialist shops. The guide has useful tips throughout, from seeking out what's free to getting off the beaten track, plus seven easy-to-follow itineraries, designed to tie together a clutch of sights in a short space of time. Add inspiring photography and detailed maps, and you've got the essential pocket-sized travel companion. **Enjoy the book, and enjoy Madeira**.

Clockwise from top: **Fortaleza de São Tiago, vintage Portugese tile, Church of Our Lady of Monte,** flowers overlooking the water, local flower, *levada* trails, sandy beach in Porto Santo

Exploring Madeira

A destination of beauty with a mild climate, this exotic island captivates with its cultural richness and exuberant landscape. Here are ideas for a two- and seven-day stay, to help you discover the island's vibrant capital, dramatic coastline and spectacular mountain scenery.

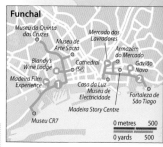

Porto Moniz

Paúl da Serra Road

Inside Funchal Cathedral there is an ornate 16th-century altarpiece.

Funchal

Museu da Quinta das Cruzes
Museu de Arte Sacra
Mercado dos Lavradores
Armazém do Mercado
Blandy's Wine Lodge
Cathedral (Sé)
Gavião Novo
Madeira Film Experience
Casa da Luz – Museu de Electricidade
Fortaleza de São Tiago
Madeira Story Centre
Museu CR7

0 metres 500
0 yards 500

Two Days in Funchal

Day ❶
MORNING

Learn about the island's history at the **Madeira Film Experience** *(see p76)*, or take a guided walking tour with **History Tellers** *(see p76)*. Kick off the sightseeing in style at the glitzy **Museu CR7** *(see p48)* and then allow at least an hour to browse the magnificent art collection at **Museu de Arte Sacra** *(see pp14–15)*.

AFTERNOON

After lunch, enjoy the exhibits at the **Museu da Quinta das Cruzes** *(see pp18–21)* before visiting **Funchal Cathedral (Sé)** *(see pp12–13)*. End the day with a pre-booked guided tour of **Blandy's Wine Lodge** *(see pp16–17)*.

Day ❷
MORNING

Join the throngs at **Mercado dos Lavradores** *(see pp24–5)*. Next, be enlightened at **Casa da Luz – Museu de Electricidade** *(see p22)*. Spend the rest of the morning absorbing the information at the fascinating **Madeira Story Centre** *(see p23)*.

AFTERNOON

Continue exploring **Zona Velha** *(see pp22–3)* and shop at **Armazém do Mercado** *(see p23)*. Finish the day by scrambling over the 17th-century **Fortaleza de São Tiago** *(see p22)* and dinner at **Gavião Novo** *(see p79)*.

Seven Days in Madeira

Days ❶ and ❷

Follow the two-day Funchal itinerary.

Day ❸

Take the cable car to **Jardim Botânico** *(see pp26–9)* via **Monte** *(see pp34–5)*. Return from Monte by a thrilling toboggan ride back into town. Later, head to the **marina** *(see p75)* for a sightseeing cruise and **whale- and dolphin-watching excursion** *(see p58)*.

Day ❹

Drive to **Pico do Arieiro** *(see pp38–9)* for spectacular mountain views. Double back to **Ribeiro Frio** *(see p83)* for lunch at the restaurant. Walk off

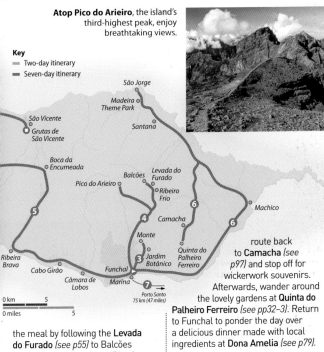

Atop Pico do Arieiro, the island's third-highest peak, enjoy breathtaking views.

Key
- Two-day itinerary
- Seven-day itinerary

the meal by following the **Levada do Furado** (see p55) to Balcões for fabulous valley views. Dine in Funchal at **Armazém do Sal** (see p79).

Day ➎

Arrive early at **Câmara de Lobos** (see p82). Marvel at the dizzying panorama from **Cabo Girão** (see p81). From **Ribeira Brava** (see p87) head inland to **Boca da Encumeada** (see p81) and take the Paúl da Serra road to **Porto Moniz** (see p88) and a lovely restaurant, **O Cachalote** (see p91). Head east to **São Vicente** (see p87) and the wonderfully evocative **Grutas de São Vicente** (see p58) before heading back.

Day ➏

Breakfast in **Machico** (see p95) and, if it's open, visit the **Capela dos Milagres** (see p47). In Santana find the iconic A-frame houses (see p82). Admire sea vistas at **São Jorge** (see p54) before visiting the family-friendly **Madeira Theme Park** (see p58). In the afternoon, opt for the scenic

route back to **Camacha** (see p97) and stop off for wickerwork souvenirs. Afterwards, wander around the lovely gardens at **Quinta do Palheiro Ferreiro** (see pp32–3). Return to Funchal to ponder the day over a delicious dinner made with local ingredients at **Dona Amelia** (see p79).

Day ➐

Embark on a leisurely day cruise to Porto Santo. In **Vila Baleira** (see p101), visit the **Casa Museu Cristóvão Colombo** (see p102). Afterwards, relax over refreshments at one of the cafés in Largo do Pelourinho. If the day is hot and sunny, head to the beach (see p52). If you'd rather explore, hire a scooter and follow the **Porto Santo itinerary** (see p103). Arrive back at Vila Baleira in time for the return cruise to Funchal.

Porto Santo beach is a glorious expanse of golden sand, ideal for sunbathing.

Top 10 Madeira Highlights

**Panoramic mountain scenery,
near Pico do Arieiro**

🔟 Madeira Highlights

Madeira is an island of contrasts: the sophistication of the capital, Funchal, compared with the primeval woodland that cloaks the island's interior, and the fertile, flower-filled gardens with the arid volcanic peaks. There are also gently rippling *levadas* (canals), and the crashing waves that dash the island's rocky shores.

1 Funchal Cathedral (Sé)

Hewn out of the island's rock and timber, Madeira's cathedral is a monument to the piety of the island's first settlers (see pp12–13).

2 Museu de Arte Sacra, Funchal

Trade contacts with Antwerp in the 15th century enabled Madeira's merchants to sell their valuable sugar and buy the Flemish works of art that fill this museum (see pp14–15).

3 Blandy's Wine Lodge, Funchal

Madeira is renowned for its wines, famous for their complexity and depth of flavour. At this historic wine lodge, you can learn to be a Madeira connoisseur (see pp16–17).

4 Museu da Quinta das Cruzes, Funchal

Look inside a gracious Madeiran mansion, built on the site of the home of the island's first ruler, João Gonçalves Zarco (see pp18–21).

5 Zona Velha

Funchal's Old Town is the city's hippest nightlife hub: a collection of buzzing bars and restaurants around Rua de Santa Maria *(see pp22–5)*.

6 Jardim Botânico, Funchal

The Botanical Gardens are a great showcase for the plants that thrive in the island's warm and humid climate, from orchids to cacti *(see pp26–9)*.

7 Quinta do Palheiro Ferreiro

Two centuries of cultivation have produced this lovely all-seasons garden where the flowers of the world blend with the English flair for garden design *(see pp32–3)*.

8 Monte

Escape to a romantic world of gardens and teahouses at this home of Emperor Charles I in exile. Return on the Monte toboggan run *(see pp34–5)*.

9 Curral das Freiras

During pirate attacks, the nuns of Santa Clara took refuge in this hidden valley encircled by sheer cliffs – a place of breath-taking beauty *(see pp36–7)*.

10 Pico do Arieiro

Feel on top of the world as you view the island's rugged, mountainous interior from the summit of Madeira's third-highest peak *(see pp38–9)*.

Funchal Cathedral (Sé)

Save for a flurry of pinnacles at the eastern end, Funchal Cathedral's exterior is very plain. By contrast, the interior is lined with statues, paintings and gold-covered chapels; the ceiling is comprised of spectacular knotwork inspired by Moorish geometry; and set in the floor are the tombs of early bishops and sugar merchants. Designed by Pêro Anes, assisted by master mason Gil Enes, the cathedral was begun in 1493. Consecrated in September 1514, when Funchal was officially granted city status, it was finally completed in October 1517.

NEED TO KNOW

MAP P3 ■ Largo da Sé
■ 291 228 155

Open 8am–noon & 4–6pm daily

■ The cathedral marks the city's social heart. The pavement cafés to the south (Funchal and Golden Gate Grand Café) are popular meeting spots for those who live in the centre, and great places to watch the world go by.

■ The cathedral is a functioning religious building, and visits are not encouraged during services (weekdays at 8am, 8:30am, 11am and 4:30pm; Sundays at 8am, 9am, 11am and 3pm). If you wish to attend a service, you will have the opportunity to see the normally dark interior of the church lit up.

1 South Transept
Sunlight floods through the transept windows to light up the timber ceiling with its everlasting knots making arabesques and stars. Faded figures around the edge of the ceiling depict Fortune holding a billowing sail, centaurs and fish-tailed mermen.

2 North Aisle
Madeira's trade links with Antwerp are reflected in an unusual 16th-century brass memorial set in the floor to the west of the first chapel. The brass shows the merchant Pedro de Brito Oliveira Pestana and his wife Catarina.

3 Baptistry
The vestibule to the church is paved in worn, 16th-century tomb slabs of black basalt. A wall plaque records the visit of Pope John Paul II on 12 May 1991. To the left is the massive 16th-century font of the Gothic baptistry.

4 Seating in the Sanctuary
Carved in 1510–11, and attributed to Flemish sculptor Olivier de Gand, the bold blue-and-gold choir stalls **(left)** depict saints, the Apostles and prophets dressed in the elaborate attire of merchants.

7 West Portal

King Manuel I of Portugal (1495–1521) helped to fund the construction of the cathedral, and therefore it is his coat of arms that appears over the Gothic doorway **(left)**. The delicate rose window set above the small crown is carved out of the rust-red local basalt.

> **KNOTWORK CEILINGS**
>
> Funchal Cathedral has one of the richest and most elaborate of Portuguese knotwork ceilings, comparable in splendour to the ceiling of the Chapel of the Royal Palace at Sintra. Funchal's delirious and dizzying pattern of knots and lozenges, with projections similar to stalactites, is based on the rich geometric art of medieval Islam. Much of Portugal was under Moorish rule from AD 711 to AD 1249.

9 East End

Go outside to the east end for the best view of the spire, and for the bravado display of barley-sugar pinnacles and pierced balustrades.

10 Sanctuary

The nautical theme continues on the gilded ceiling of the sanctuary, where a carving of an armillary sphere (a navigation aid) is among the painted cherubs and floral swags.

5 Altarpiece

The sizeable altarpiece **(above)** was made in the early 16th century. Set within its ornate Gothic frames are 12 scenes from the lives of Christ and the Virgin.

8 Ceiling

Madeira's native white cedar trees were used to brilliant effect in the construction of the ceiling of the nave, aisles and transepts. It is one of the finest examples in Portugal of *alfarge*, or "knotwork", a technique blending Moorish and European elements.

6 Nave and South Aisle

In this area **(right)**, there are many floor memorials to bishops and merchants. Carved in marble and basalt, they reflect the 16th-century Portuguese style.

🔟 ⭐ Museu de Arte Sacra, Funchal

Madeira is not the first place you would think of to look for some of the finest Flemish masterpieces, but the 15th-century sugar trade between Funchal and Antwerp (in modern Belgium) provides the link. Merchants and plantation owners commissioned altarpieces showing themselves and their families. Thus the colourful paintings in this museum of religious art are also portraits of some of the first settlers.

① St Philip and St James by Pieter Coecke van Aelst

Here the donors, pictured kneeling either side of the central panel **(above)**, are Simão Gonçalves de Câmara, grandson of Zarco, and his wife Isabel.

② Processional Cross

This exquisite silverwork **(right)** was donated at the dedication of Funchal's cathedral in 1514 by King Manuel I of Portugal (1495–1521). Gothic niches are filled with tiny figures of saints and scenes from the Passion and Crucifixion.

③ Entrance Hall

The importance of the bishop in local life is reflected in his elegant palace, which is now the museum. Visitors enter via a handsome hall floored with pebbles forming swags and garlands. A Baroque stone staircase, from the 1750s, is flanked by gilded candelabra.

④ The Machico Adoration

This anonymous painting of around 1518 from the church at Machico (see p95) depicts in detail Madeiran merchants and landowners in the guise of the Three Kings.

⑤ Annunciation by Joost van Cleve

The results of Europe's expanding trade connections can be seen in this serene painting of around 1515: Mary's feet rest on an oriental carpet, and the lilies symbolizing her purity stand in a Delft jar.

6 The Last Supper Tableau

This almost life-size wooden tableau **(above)** was carved for the cathedral in 1648 by Manuel Pereira. Judas sits alone clutching a money bag.

7 St Sebastian

This painted stone statue **(right)**, carved by Diogo Pires in the early 16th-century, is full of holes that once held arrows. St Sebastian, the Roman martyr, was condemned to death for his faith. He survived the arrows, but was later beheaded.

8 Deposition by Gerard David

The Virgin's face shows resignation in the central panel **(below)** of this triptych of 1518. Side panels depict Simon Acciaiuoli, a merchant from Florence (with St Bernardino of Siena), and his wife Maria (with St James) – the donors.

9 St James by Dieric Bouts

A study of St James, probably painted in Bruges in the 1470s, shows the saint's scarlet cloak. This and the flower-filled meadow in which he stands are typical of Flemish master Dieric Bouts' colour and naturalistic detail.

10 St Anne and St Joachim

This fascinating early 16th-century painting **(right)** of the Antwerp School is said to show King Ladislaw III of Poland *(see p43)* and his wife Senhorinha Eanes. Portuguese tradition has it that the king gave up his crown after the Battle of Varna and settled on Madeira in 1454, where he was known as Henry the German.

FLEMISH ART

Madeiran art patrons would probably not have visited Antwerp or Bruges to sit for their portraits. Instead, they might have sent a sketch (perhaps drawn by one of the island's architects or masons) or perhaps relied on a friend to give the artist an accurate verbal description. In any case, creating an exact likeness was not the artist's aim. Following the Mannerist tendency, the painter of the Machico *Adoration* emphasizes distinctive facial features – a large nose, a double chin, a prominent forehead – in order to give character to his subjects.

NEED TO KNOW

MAP P3 ■ Rua do Bispo 21 ■ 291 228 900 ■ www. masf.pt/homepage.html

Open 10am–5pm Tue–Sat

Adm €5 (under 12s free)

■ The Renaissance loggia facing onto Praça do Município is now the chic Café do Museu. A great place for a snack, lunch or early evening meal, the café serves salads, pasta dishes, homemade soups and light meals from 10am to 6pm Mon–Fri.

TOP 10 ★ Blandy's Wine Lodge, Funchal

With its heavy ancient beams and cobblestone courtyards, Blandy's Wine Lodge can provide a solid introduction to the history of its unique wine. It is set in the surviving parts of a 17th-century Franciscan friary, most of which was demolished when Portugal passed its laws banning religious orders in 1834. The premises were acquired by the Blandy family in 1840 and have been used ever since for making Madeira wine.

NEED TO KNOW

MAP P3 ■ Avenida Arriaga 28 ■ 291 228 978 ■ www.blandyswine lodge.com

Open 10am–6:30pm Mon–Fri

Premium Tour: 10:30am, 2:30pm, 3:30pm & 4:30pm Mon–Fri; €10.50; Vintage Tour: 4:30pm Mon–Fri; €21.80

■ Premium Tour is also conducted in German, French, Portuguese and Spanish – see website for schedule.

■ Wines can be sampled in the Max Römer Tasting Bar, and all the wines, including vintages, are payable by the glass. The cost is refundable when you buy a bottle (except for vintage and package tours).

■ There is an outdoor café in the São Francisco friary, which is now a lovely public garden.

1 Max Römer Tasting Bar
The lovely sunny murals **(above)** of grape-growing and harvesting that cover the walls of the tasting bar on the ground floor were painted in 1922 by the German artist Max Römer (1878–1960).

2 Attics
Massive timbers support three storeys of ventilated attics. Wines here are aged in casks warmed only by the sun, a method known as *canteiro* that is used to produce quality wines.

Vintage Room 3
Within the Vintage Room **(right)**, precious wines are stored by date and kept behind bars. Madeira wines dating back to the early 20th century can be sampled here. Or it may be worth trying more moderately priced, but still appealing, vintages from the 1980s.

4 Courtyard
The romantic inner courtyard of the wine lodge is shaded by some of the island's tallest banana trees **(above)**. It is ringed by three storeys of attics with wisteria-draped balconies.

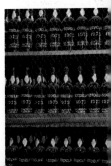

7 Wine Museum
Framed letters of appreciation from kings and queens, emperors, presidents and prime ministers – all lovers of Madeira wine – line the walls of the museum at the heart of the lodge. Also on display here are leather-bound ledgers **(left)** recording sales as far back as the 1700s.

MADEIRA WINE

Madeira wine has two defining characteristics. First, it is "fortified" by the addition of brandy at the final stage of the fermentation process. Second, it is heated as it ages in a process known as *estufagem (see p63)*. The benefits of heating were discovered when wines left on board ship after a round trip to the equator were found to have developed a new depth and complexity of flavour. Winemakers worked out how to re-create this by ageing the wine in hothouses.

9 18th-Century Wine Press
A traditional 18th-century wine press **(below)** with the Jesuit symbol of a cross within a triangle is displayed in the courtyard. The Jesuits managed the island's wine trade until the late 18th century. Then English and Scottish merchants took it over.

5 The "Oldest Street"
The street that runs up the eastern side of the wine lodge dates from the 1400s. In the early days of settlement, wine barrels were dragged across the cobbles on a sledge to the harbour.

6 Ageing Room
In the ageing room visitors will find the satin wood vats that contain the wine as it matures. These massive vats are more than 100 years old and can hold more than 9,000 litres (1,980 gallons). The wine is stored here before it is bottled.

8 Wine Shop
This contemporary shop stocks a large selection of wines by producers from the Madeira Wine Company; as well as Madeiran liqueurs, Portuguese table wines and spirits.

10 Goatskins
Wine made all over the island was brought for sale to Funchal. Porters called *borracheiros* sipped from the 40-litre loads of wine that they carried in goatskins.

TOP 10 ⭐ Museu da Quinta das Cruzes, Funchal

Madeira's early settlers built their homes on the heights above the harbour so that they could see pirate ships approaching. The Quinta das Cruzes is one such estate. Originally built by Captain Zarco, it was later rebuilt as the elegant home of the Lomelino family, and is now a museum full of decorative artwork. A visit can be combined with a stroll to the Convento de Santa Clara nearby.

3 Orchid Garden

A stately old dragon tree *(see p27)* thrusts its fleshy limbs through the roof of the shade house at the rear of the *quinta* garden, where tier upon tier of exquisite tropical orchids are cultivated for use as cut flowers.

1 Archaeological Park

The gardens to the south of the *quinta* **(above)** serve as an outdoor museum of archaeological remains. One prominent piece is the tombstone of João Rodrigues de Freitas (c 1436–1523), a Portuguese navigator and one of the first Madeiran settlers.

Museu da Quinta das Cruzes floorplan

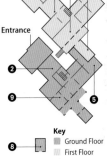

Entrance

Key
Ground Floor
First Floor

NEED TO KNOW

MAP N2

Museu da Quinta das Cruzes: Calçada do Pico 1; open 10am–5:30pm Tue–Sat; adm €3; mqc. madeira.gov.pt

Convento de Santa Clara: Calçada de Santa Clara 15; 291 742 602; closed for renovation; adm €2

■ The museum's café-restaurant has beautiful bay views.

■ The ticket office will have details of concerts held at the museum.

■ It's a steep climb to the museum but taxis and the Route Eco bus also come up here.

2 Silver Collection

The rich collection of historic silver reflects the predominant trends in Europe from the 16th to the 19th century. The highlights are a golden-silver 16th-century pax and two silver and coral British baby's rattles.

4 Drawing Rooms

Zarco's mansion was a working farm and administrative centre, remodelled by the Lomelino family in the 18th and 19th centuries. Furniture and paintings in the drawing rooms **(left)** were influenced by the British style of the period.

5 Sugar Box Furniture

Brazilian sugar put an end to the Madeiran trade. The cupboards in the basement were made from the wooden boxes used to carry the sugar.

8 Chapel

The chapel, dating from 1692, contains the tomb of Urbano Lomelino, an early sugar merchant who migrated to the island from Italy in the early 1500s.

CAPTAIN ZARCO: LORD OF THE ISLES

João Gonçalves, who was nicknamed Zarco ("Squinter") after he lost an eye in battle in 1415, planted the Portuguese flag on Porto Santo in 1419, and on Madeira in 1420. In 1425, he returned with people, seeds and tools to live on Madeira. Zarco ruled the island's southwestern half, while fellow captain Tristão Vaz Teixeira ruled the northeast from Machico. Zarco's half proved to have the better harbour, Funchal, which later became the capital. He died in 1467 in Funchal (see p42).

9 Palanquin

A 19th-century palanquin, used to carry wealthy ladies around Funchal, is displayed on the ground floor. There is also a series of English satirical engravings poking fun at Funchal's well-fed priests and overdressed officials.

10 Artwork by Tomás da Anunciação

Picnic **(below)**, by the founder of Portuguese Romanticism, dates from 1865. The family of the second Count of Carvalhal is shown on their Quinta do Palheiro Ferreiro estate (see pp32–3).

6 Manueline Windows

The stone window frames **(above)** set in the garden are fine examples of a style inspired by the voyages of discovery made during the reign of King Manuel I of Portugal (1495–1521). They are carved with ships' ropes, leaves, other flora and lions.

7 Exhibitions

The museum also hosts a permanent exhibition of decorative arts dating from the 15th to the 19th centuries, which encompasses paintings, sculpture, ceramics, jewellery and furniture, including a display of 19th-century drawings and watercolours of Madeira.

Convento de Santa Clara, Funchal

The cloister at the Convento de Santa Clara

1 Cloister

This peaceful spot provided access to chapels and oratories, where the nuns could pass the day in prayer. Admire the cupola of the convent's bell tower from here, decorated with rare 17th-century blue, white and gold ceramic tiles.

2 Abbess's Grave

A gravestone with Gothic script marks the burial place of the convent's first abbess, Isabel de Noronha, and her sister, Constança. As a sign of their humility, these two high-born ladies, whose grandfather was Zarco (see p19), chose to be buried in a corridor where the nuns would walk across their graves each day.

Convento de Santa Clara floorplan

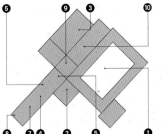

3 Gateway

The arms of the Order of St Francis are carved on the 17th-century stone roundel above the ancient wooden doors of the convent gateway. Ring the bell here to enter.

4 Lower Choir

The lower choir is lined with wooden choir stall chairs dating from 1736, carved with cherubs and amusing animal heads. The painted throne was reserved for the use of the bishop and the head of the Franciscan order when they visited.

5 Grille

Through the iron grille in the eastern wall of the lower choir, the congregation could hear the singing of the nuns, and the nuns could hear the priest say mass. The nuns had no other contact with the outside world.

6 Zarco Monument

A coffin-shaped box at the end of the lower choir is a replica of the marble tombstone that stood over Zarco's grave (see p19). It was moved because priests kept tripping over it.

7 Upper Choir

Green Moorish tiles cover the floor of this long room, with its *alfarge* (knotwork) ceiling and gilded altar housing a statue of the Virgin. This choir was the place of daily prayer for the first community of Poor Clare nuns (the sister order to the Franciscans), who came to Santa Clara from Portugal in 1497.

8 Calvary

The large painting of the crucified Christ at the west end of the lower choir served to remind the nuns that their hardships were as nothing compared with his sufferings. Even more poignant is the realistic 17th-century statue of Christ laid in the altar below, as if in his tomb.

9 Monuments

At the back of the church, the stone sarcophagus resting on crouching lions marks the grave of Zarco's son-in-law, Martim Mendes de Vasconcelos (d.1493). Zarco *(see p19)* himself, who died in 1467, lies buried in front of the high altar, but his tomb slab is hidden beneath a modern wood floor.

10 Church

Santa Clara Church boasts one of Madeira's finest religious interiors, and it can be admired without visiting the rest of the convent. The public part of the church is covered in decorative 17th-century carpet tiles of great intricacy. The magnificent silver tabernacle on the altar dates from 1671.

Tiles on the ceiling of the church

SANTA CLARA CHURCH

Santa Clara Convent is surrounded by high walls, built to shield the nuns from prying eyes and keep them focused on their religious duties without the distractions of the outside world. In the past, the only part of the convent open to the public was the church, with its magnificent silver tabernacle, dating from 1671, and wooden altar, painted to imitate marble and gold. Serene and beautiful, Santa Clara Church is a popular choice for weddings.

**TOP 10
DATES IN SANTA CLARA'S HISTORY**

1 1476: convent founded

2 1493: church completed

3 1497: nuns move in

4 1566: nuns flee pirates

5 1671: tabernacle unveiled

6 1736: choir stalls carved

7 1797: artists paint church

8 1834: Portugal bans religious orders

9 1890: last nun dies

10 1927: school founded

Secluded and graceful, Santa Clara Convent has preserved some historical treasures.

TOP 10 ⭐ Zona Velha, Funchal

With its choice of lively bars and cafés, celebrated restaurants and compelling visitor attractions, Funchal's Zona Velha (Old Town) is a rejuvenated destination. Centred around ancient, cobbled Rua de Santa Maria, in the early 19th century the neighbourhood was an industrious centre of trade and commerce. Allowed to fall into disrepair and for many years neglected, the maze of narrow streets and their long-abandoned merchants' warehouses once again form a vibrant social hub, complemented by proud local tradition and a fascinating collection of historical and cultural landmarks.

Art of Open Doors ①

Rua de Santa Maria features some amazing examples of street art **(right)**. Local artists have painted over many of the neighbourhood's doors, producing art ranging from quirky cartoon murals to abstract designs. There are also examples of sculpture.

② Museu do Brinquedo

Inside the Armazém do Mercado, this toy museum features 20,000 examples of cars, games and dolls donated by José Manuel Borges Pereira and other collectors. The antique items are fascinating. Look out too for rare Star Wars and Action Man collectibles.

④ Jardim do Almirante Reis

This attractive green space fronting Zona Velha is divided into undulating lawns crossed by footpaths. During the summer the garden often hosts arts and crafts fairs and other cultural events.

③ Fortaleza de São Tiago

Situated above the seafront is this early-17th-century fortress *(see p67)*, instantly recognizable by its chunky, ochre walls **(below)**. Built to defend the port from pirate attack, the stronghold's castellated battlements, turrets and hidden rooms make for intriguing exploration.

⑤ Casa da Luz – Museu de Electricidade

Definitely one to spark the imagination of both adults and kids, the Electricity Museum is set within the city's old power station. Gleaming like new, massive diesel generators stand downstairs while the first floor has a fun, interactive, multimedia "energy sources" exhibition.

7 Madeira Story Centre

The first stop for visitors to Madeira is this inter-active museum **(left)** that describes the island's history and culture, from its volcanic origins to the present day. The impressive exhibition, arranged chronologically, takes a good hour to absorb. Relax afterwards at the rooftop restaurant.

FUNCHAL'S DOOR ART

In 2010 Spanish artist José Maria Zyberchema launched the Art of Open Doors project by using a derelict door in Rua de Santa Maria as a canvas for a mural. A way of brightening up a run-down neighbourhood soon blossomed into permanent street art.

9 Capela do Corpo Santo

The exterior **(below)** of this plain mid-16th-century chapel *(see p67)* does not promise much, but once inside the sacred artworks adorning the walls and ceiling are impressive. The portal dates from the 15th century.

6 Armazém do Mercado

The "Market Warehouse" was created in a former embroidery factory. The pop-up space has artisan boutiques and eateries.

8 Cable Car

The Jardim do Almirante Reis *teleférico* station is the start of the spectacular ride up to Monte *(see pp34–5)*. Kids under six go free.

10 Mercado dos Lavradores

Funchal's busy "Farmers' Market" *(see pp24–5)* is an attractive riot of sound and colour, especially on Saturday mornings.

NEED TO KNOW

Art of Open Doors: **MAP P4–5**; www. arteportasabertas.com

Museu do Brinquedo: **MAP P4**; Rua L Coelho 39; adm; www.armazem domercado.com/museu

Casa da Luz – Museu de Electricidade: **MAP Q4**;

Rua Casa da Luz 2; 291 211 480; open 10am–12:30pm 2–6pm Tue–Sat; adm €2.70 (under 12s free)

Armazém do Mercado: **MAP P4**; Rua do Hospital Velho 28; open 10am–7pm Mon–Fri (to 2pm Sat); www. armazemdomercado.com

Madeira Story Centre: **MAP P5**; Rua D Carlos I 27–29;

open 9am–7pm daily; www. madeirastorycentre.com

Capela do Corpo Santo: **MAP H6**; Largo do Corpo Santo; open 10am–12:30pm, 2–5pm Mon–Fri

Mercado dos Lavradores: **MAP P4**; Largo dos Lavradores; open 8am–7pm Mon–Thu, 7am–8pm Fri (to 2pm Sat)

Mercado dos Lavradores, Funchal

Painted blue tiles depicting Leda and the Swan

1 Leda and the Swan
To the right of the entrance porch, a tile picture shows the market as it was at the turn of the 20th century, with canvas awnings and stallholders in traditional costume. The fountain in the picture, topped by a marble statue of *Leda and the Swan* (1880), is now in the town hall *(see p44)* courtyard.

2 Flower Sellers
Today's flower sellers still wear traditional clothes. Their outfits are as colourful and eye-catching as their tropical orchids, bird-of-paradise plants, lilies and flamingo flowers.

3 Butchers and Bars
The butchers' shops, selling fresh, cooked and dried meat and sausages, are in a separate area reached from streets around the market hall. Ringing the perimeter of the hall are hole-in-the-wall bars, where shoppers and market workers snack on little dishes of lupin beans, salty olives or sweet custard pastries.

4 The Market Hall
This Art Deco hall was originally designed in 1937 by Edmundo Tavares (1892–1983). Though it has been built from modern materials, its colours echo the grey and rust-red basalt of traditional Madeiran architecture.

5 Chocolate
Sample delicious artisanal chocolate infused with traditional Madeiran flavours at the

A riot of colourful flowers for sale

Uau Cacau stand. Make sure to try the award-winning passion fruit truffle and the hot chocolate. The company also has a shop near Funchal's Cathedral *(see p46)*.

6 Tile Pictures

More tile pictures adorn the entrance porch. The work of artist João Rodrigues, made in 1940, depicts stallholders and the coat of arms of Funchal (featuring five sugar cones in a cross).

7 Fruit and Vegetables

Upstairs is the domain of the fruit and vegetable sellers, and it is packed with all manner of colourful and sweet-smelling local produce. As you negotiate the narrow aisles, don't be surprised to be offered a free slice of mango, a passion fruit or a blood-red tomarillo by the stall holders as you pass, in the hope that you will linger and buy.

8 Fish Market

Set in the basement, this noisy fish market exemplifies the island's ancient relationship with the sea through its vast array of fish and seafood, including fresh cuts of tuna, plump ocean bream and black *espada* (scabbard fish).

Stalls selling produce at the market

9 Ground Floor

In the arcades surrounding the central courtyard, you can shop for leather bags and wickerwork, *fado* CDs, Madeira wine and honey cake. Farmers down from the country for the day sell bread, bunches of herbs and seasonal fruits from upturned crates.

10 Herbalist

On the first floor near the stairs, there is a stall devoted to selling fresh and dried herbs, all carefully labelled. There are bunches of feverfew for headaches, and fennel and eucalyptus sweets to soothe a cold.

THE FRUITS OF MADEIRA

In Funchal's market, even the commonplace can take you by surprise: the tiny honey-scented bananas, no bigger than your finger, are the best you will ever taste. Ignore shiny imported apples and tomatoes in favour of flavoursome varieties that have been grown on the island for centuries. Try locally grown sugar cane, quince, prickly pears, loquats, custard apples, guava, *pitanga* (Brazilian cherries), pawpaw, passion fruit and pomegranate.

Many exotic fruits are sold in Madeira, including these durians and mandarins.

TOP 10 ⭐ Jardim Botânico, Funchal

As well as being a place where avid plant lovers can learn all about the astonishing range of plants that thrive in Madeira's warm and humid climate, this is also a great spot just to relax and enjoy the visual richness of the immaculately maintained flower beds. The gardens occupy the grounds of an estate that once belonged to the Reid family (founders of the world-renowned Reid's Palace) and, with a practised eye for a good location, they chose to build their mansion on a sunny slope blessed with panoramic views.

Carpet Bedding

The purple, red, green, yellow, white and gold diamonds, lozenges and circles of this much-photographed part of the estate's garden **(right)** demonstrate the great richness and variety of colour to be found just in the leaves of plants.

2 Natural History Museum

The Quinta do Bom Sucesso ("Mansion of Good Fortune"), built in the late 19th century by the Reid family *(see p43)*, was bought by the Madeiran government in 1952. In 1982, the Natural History Museum opened here.

Map of Jardim Botânico

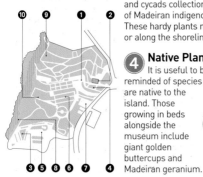

3 Coastal Plants

Near to this area, where the palm trees and cycads collection is situated, is a small group of Madeiran indigenous and endemic plant species. These hardy plants manage to thrive on rocky cliffs or along the shoreline.

4 Native Plants

It is useful to be reminded of species that are native to the island. Those growing in beds alongside the museum include giant golden buttercups and Madeiran geranium.

5 Parrot Park

The closer you get to the southern part of the garden, the less you will be able to avoid the squawks of the rare and exotic birds **(left)** that are housed in the Parrot Park.

7 Topiary Garden

This knot garden **(left)** is made of clipped box, and planted with shrubs that can be cut into spirals, pyramids, chess pieces and a variety of animal shapes.

8 Economic Plants

If you cannot tell a mango tree from an avocado, this is the place to learn. The plants grown here are used for food, fibre, oil or dye. Among the examples are several familiar names, such as coffee, cocoa, sugar cane and cotton.

9 Valley View

The western edge of the garden (furthest from the entrance) has views over the green, canyon-like João Gomes Valley. Though crossed by a road bridge, this is an important wildlife corridor. Huge, ancient parasol pines, with twisted branches and scaly bark, cling to the rocks beside the viewing point *(miradouro)*.

6 Cacti and Succulents

This part of the garden is popular with children for its Wild West look **(below)** and for the many spiders that use the thorns of the cacti as supports for their intricate webs.

DRAGON TREES

If ever a plant looked like its name, the dragon tree *(Dracaena draco)* is it. The fleshlike branches are covered in scaly grey bark that looks and feels rather reptilian, while the leaves are like claws or talons. When cut, the tree "bleeds" a vivid red sap which sets to form a resinous gum known as Dragon's Blood, once highly prized as a dye (it turns cloth purple) and harvested by sailors.

10 Scientific Plants

Staff carry out research using the plants grown in this section to better understand plant taxonomy, reproductive biology and ecology.

NEED TO KNOW

MAP H5 ■ Quinta do Bom Sucesso, Caminho do Meio ■ 291 211 200 ■ www.ifcn.madeira. gov.pt

Open 9am–5:30pm daily

Adm €6 (under 6s free)

....

■ There is a café set around pretty lotus- and lily-filled ponds.

■ Some of the best views are to be had from the "Lovers' Cave" at the top of the garden.

■ Entry to the Jardim Botânico also includes admission to the Jardim dos Loiros, or Parrot Park. Orchid fans shouldn't miss the Jardim Orquídea, a short, steep walk away.

■ A cable car gets you to Monte *(see pp34–5)* in around ten minutes.

Plants on Madeira

Native Madeiran geraniums

1 Madeiran Geranium
Also known as cranesbill, the Madeiran geranium *(Geranium maderense)* has become a popular garden plant all over Europe because of its shrubby stature, feathery leaves and large purple-veined magenta flowers.

2 Stink Laurel
The Portuguese took a heavy toll on the huge and ancient laurel trees *(Ocotea foetens,* or *til* in Portuguese) after they arrived on the island in 1420. Felled trunks were shipped to Portugal and Spain for shipbuilding; the ships of the Spanish Armada were largely built from this wood.

3 Giant Buttercups
Madeira's subtropical climate seems to encourage plants to turn into giants. Here, poinsettias grow 4 m (12 ft) tall, and heaths are trees rather than shrubs. This tall shrubby buttercup *(Ranunculus cortusifolius)* is a very handsome plant that looks good anywhere.

4 Madeiran Juniper
Confusingly called *cedro* (cedar) in Portuguese, the dark wood of the Madeiran juniper has a rich patina that can be readily seen in the knotwork ceilings of Funchal Cathedral *(see p13)*, Santa Clara Convent *(see p21)* and the church in Calheta *(see p88)*.

5 Lily-of-the-valley Tree
You could pass this shrub *(Clethra arborea,* or *folhado* in Portuguese) 9 months out of 12 and not even notice it, but from August to October it is a stunning sight, hung all over with sweet-smelling clusters of bell-like flowers of the purest white.

6 Tree Heath
Related to heather, and with similar pink bell-like flowers, Madeira's tree heaths *(Erica arborea)*

Stink laurel or *til* trees

can grow to a quite prodigious size; a carbonized tree heath trunk in Madeira's Natural History Museum *(see p26)* probably lived for several hundred years. Tree heath branches are used locally for fencing and windbreaks.

7 Scented Bay

The essential flavouring ingredient in Madeira's national dish, *espetada* (beef kebabs) is the scented bay (*Laurus novocanariensis*, or *loureiro* in Portuguese). It has aromatic evergreen leaves and grows abundantly in the wild.

8 Ironwood

Apollonias barbujana (known as *barbusano* in Portuguese) is one of the main constituents of Madeira's native evergreen forest. Its billowing clouds of fresh lime-green coloured leaves contrast pleasingly with the deep green of the previous years' growth of foliage.

9 Pride of Madeira

The plant Pride of Madeira (*Echium candicans*) is almost the symbol of the island. Blooming with an abundance of long-lasting powder-blue flower spikes at exactly the time of year (from December to March) when other flowers are usually shy, it adorns the island's roadsides.

Pride of Madeira bloom

10 Madeiran Mahogany

Madeira's museums are full of fine furniture made from *vinhático* (*Persea indica*), the mahogany-like wood that grows to a great height and girth in the woods. So valuable and costly was sugar in the 15th century that it was shipped to Europe in chests made of this wood.

MADEIRA: WORLD HERITAGE SITE

The primeval woodland that cloaks much of Madeira's mountainous interior is the remnant of the scented laurel forest that covered much of southern Europe until the last Ice Age (which ended around 10,000 years ago). Only on Madeira, the Canaries, the Azores and in tropical west Africa was the climate warm enough for these subtropical trees and shrubs to survive. Known in Portuguese as *laurissilva* (laurel wood), they are a precious link with the past. UNESCO designated a large area of the island's natural forest as a protected World Heritage Site in December 1999.

**TOP 10
WILD PLANTS TO
SPOT ON A WALK**

1 Viper's bugloss
2 Saucer plant (House leek)
3 Navelwort
4 Downy thistle
5 Shrubby sow thistle
6 Ice plant
7 Bilberry
8 Foxglove
9 Dog violet
10 Fleabane

Madeira has a wealth of plants to look out for. These include succulents such as this bright green ornamental aeonium.

Following pages The central lake in Monte Palace Tropical Garden

🔟⭐ Quinta do Palheiro Ferreiro

The unmistakably English character of the Quinta do Palheiro Ferreiro was stamped on the estate by its first owner, the wealthy Count of Carvalhal, whose love of English landscapes led him to include woodland and grassy meadows when the estate was laid out in 1804. Bought by John Blandy, an English wine merchant, in 1885, the *quinta* has remained in the same family ever since, enriched by the plants that Mildred Blandy imported from China, Japan and her native South Africa.

Sunken Garden ①

Water lilies fill the little pool at the centre of this pretty garden **(right)**. Tall cypresses mark its corners; a variety of topiary shapes flank its four sets of stone steps. In the borders, gazanias mix with beetroot-red house leeks.

Lady's Garden ②

The *Jardim da Senhora* has topiary nesting birds and vintage trees, including a grand old Madeiran *til* tree *(see p28)*, two Canary pines and a weeping *Sophora japonica*, whose spiral limbs and delicate leaves cascade down to form a natural green veil.

Chapel ③

The small, striking Baroque chapel **(left)** has Venetian-style windows and a plasterwork ceiling depicting the baptism of Christ in the River Jordan by John the Baptist.

Camellia Walk ④

Look out for the stone circle called Avista Navios (meaning "Place for Viewing Ships"), where there is a clear view all the way down to the harbour.

NEED TO KNOW

MAP H5 ▪ Caminho da Quinta do Palheiro 32, São Gonçalo ▪ 291 793 044 ▪ www.palheiro natureestate.com

Open 9am–5pm daily

Adm €11 (children 15–17s €5, under 15s free)

▪ The Tea House is at the end of the garden, near an area now run as a golf course *(see p57)*.

▪ A rose garden, near the chapel, has traditional roses and newer varieties brought in from the UK.

▪ Casa Velha is open to hotel guests only.

7 Terrace

Paved with tiny sea-worn pebbles, the terrace **(above)** offers a good view of the house (no admission) that John Blandy built in 1885. He managed successfully to blend the English and the Madeiran architectural styles.

Map of Quinta do Palheiro Ferreiro

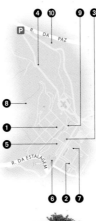

8 Hell Valley

Despite its name, this valley is a delightful tangle of bamboo, tree ferns, native woodland and creepers, with an understorey of beautiful acanthus plants.

9 Stream Garden

The stream you cross to enter the garden is fed by a spring that attracts birds. Lined by azaleas, rhododendrons and scarlet tritonias, it is crossed by pretty bridges.

5 Long Borders

Typically English herbaceous border plants, such as delphiniums and day lilies, are mixed with tender and exotic orchids, and angel's trumpets (daturas). Climbing roses and jasmine hang over arches so that you catch their scent as you pass.

10 Long Avenue

Plane trees and giant camellias, many planted 200 years ago, line the avenue. The red, pink and white flowers are at their best from November to April, before white arum lilies and blue agapanthus take over.

Casa Velha 6

Now a luxurious hotel (see p114–15), the "old house" **(right)** was originally a hunting lodge. Archduchess Leopoldina of Austria stayed here on her way to marry Pedro I of Brazil in 1817.

TOP 10 ⭐ Monte

Monte (literally, "Mount") developed in the late 18th century as a genteel and healthy retreat from the heat, smells, noise and commercial activity of the capital. Funchal's suburbs now spread all the way up to Monte, but there is still a sense of escaping from the city and entering a world set apart. The cool, clear air is filled with birdsong. Few cars intrude onto the cobbled streets, and lush gardens can be found everywhere – lushest of all, the extraordinary Monte Palace Tropical Garden.

1 Monte Palace Tropical Garden

Lakes, waterfalls and an engaging museum have earned the Monte Palace Tropical Garden (above) a name among the most beautiful botanical gardens in the world.

3 Quinta Jardins do Imperador

Just south of Monte is the beautiful mansion where Austrian Emperor Charles I lived in exile. The knot gardens and lake enclose the Malakoff Tower, which houses a café.

4 Monte Cable Car

The cable car's sleek terminus is Monte's only modern building. Along its route up the wild João Gomes Valley, you can see examples of many protected species of native trees and flowers.

2 Toboggan Run

Monte's toboggans (right) are steered by smartly dressed *carreiros* (toboggan drivers) in straw boaters on the 2-km (1-mile) trip from Monte to Livramento.

8 Church Steps

On the Feast of the Assumption (15 August), pilgrims climb on their knees up the steps **(left)** to Monte's church to pay homage to the statue of the Virgin. They believe the statue was given by the Virgin when she appeared to a shepherd girl in the 15th century.

5 Parque do Monte

This public park was laid out in 1894 under the railway viaduct draped in *Monstera deliciosa* plants. Cobbled paths lead into a valley of hydrangeas, tree ferns and agapanthus.

9 House of the Pilgrims

This 18th-century building is now used as a cultural centre. It houses an exhibition of paintings devoted to the Emperor Charles I who lived in exile here.

6 Fountain Square

Located in a natural amphitheatre shaded by giant plane trees, Monte's main square is artfully paved with sea-rounded cobbles. The square is named after the marble *fonte* of 1897. In its back wall is a niche housing a statue of the Virgin of Monte – a copy of the one in the church.

10 Quinta do Monte

Converted into a fine hotel (*see p114*), the 19th-century Quinta do Monte sits in beautiful terraced grounds, open to the public during the day. At the heart of the garden is the Baroque chapel **(above)** of the Quinta do Monte. In the garden gazebo is a small café serving teas.

7 Nossa Senhora do Monte

Our Lady of Monte was inaugurated in 1818, replacing a 15th-century chapel built by Adam Ferreira (the first person to be born on Madeira – along with his twin sister, Eve). The church houses the tomb of Emperor Charles I of Austria.

EMPEROR CHARLES I (1887–1922)

Charles I was ruler of an empire that occupied most of central Europe. When it collapsed with Austria's defeat in World War I, he fled into exile, eventually ending up on Madeira, from where the British thought he would be unlikely to try and retake the throne. Arriving on the island in November 1921, he suffered pneumonia and died in April 1922. He was beatified by Pope John Paul II, and pilgrims now regularly visit his tomb in Monte's church.

NEED TO KNOW
MAP H5

Monte Palace Tropical Garden: Caminho do Monte; open 9:30am–6pm daily; adm €12.50 (under 15s free); www.montepalace.com

Toboggan Run: open 10am–5pm Mon–Sat; fare €25 (€30 for two people, €45 for three)

Quinta Jardins do Imperador: Caminho do Pico; 291 630 458; open 9:30am–5:30pm Mon–Sat, 10:30am–5:30pm Sun; adm €1 (under 12s free)

Monte Cable Car: www.telefericodofunchal.com

Nossa Senhora do Monte: 291 783 877; open 9am–6:30pm Fri to 7pm Sat, 7:30am–6pm Sun

■ From Funchal take bus 20 or 21 or the cable car from Zona Velha or Jardim Botânico. Return on the Monte toboggan or on foot down Caminho do Monte.

TOP 10 ⭐ Curral das Freiras

To get a feel for the grandeur of Madeira's mountainous interior visit Curral das Freiras ("Nuns' Refuge"), the hidden valley used by the nuns of Santa Clara Convent whenever pirates attacked the island. There is a little village that now nestles there. From such a beautiful spot, the nuns must have returned to their city convent with a heavy heart. Visiting in 1825, H N Coleridge (the nephew of the English poet) described the Curral as "one of the great sights of the world".

1 Road

Until the road **(below)** was built in 1969, the only way into the valley was the footpath. The old road is now closed and a modern tunnelled highway connects the valley with the rest of the island.

2 East View

Because of its cauldron-like shape, early explorers thought the Curral das Freiras, with its dramatic cliffs rising sheer to the east, was a collapsed volcano. In fact, the circular form is the result of millions of years of river and rain erosion.

3 Chestnut Woods

The descent to the village takes you through chestnut woods. The trees bear white, sweetly scented flower stems in August, and produce edible chestnuts in October. Lower down, there is natural *laurissilva* forest *(see p29)*. In June, look out for wild orchids.

4 Miradouro

From the car park in front of the hotel, a short footpath leads up to a *miradouro*, or viewing point **(right)**, located high above the Socorridos Valley. From this spot, the village far down below looks like "Shangri-La" – the utopia of James Hilton's novel *Lost Horizon* (1933).

Igreja Matriz ⑤

The church in Curral das Freiras dates from the early 19th century. On the last Sunday in August, a statue of the church's patron saint is carried through streets festooned throughout with colourful flags (**right**) and paper flowers.

Eira do Serrado ⑧

Admiring this vista from Eira do Serrado (**left**) is as much a part of a visit to Curral das Freiras as the descent into the village itself. There is a hotel and restaurant, so if you love the romantic view, you can stay for lunch or dinner, or even spend the night (*see p116*).

West View ⑨

To the west is a serrated ridge with three prominent peaks: Pico do Cavalo, Pico do Serradinho and, highest of all at 1,654 m (5,427 ft), Pico Grande. The next big valley runs from Ribeira Brava to São Vicente via Encumeada Pass.

Footpath ⑥

You can walk down to the village along the cobbled footpath that begins in the car park. The path has 52 bends; at the bottom, turn right and walk up to the village. You can return by bus 81.

North View ⑦

To the north, a road heads up the valley, ending just after it disappears from view. There are plans for a tunnel to take the road to the north coast, risking the Curral's tranquillity.

NEED TO KNOW

MAP G4 ■ www.horarios dofunchal.pt

■ At Sabores do Curral (*see p85*), delicious local cuisine is served on a terrace with spectacular mountain views.

■ Many tour companies in Funchal offer half-day trips to Curral das Freiras, often including Monte (*see p34*) or Câmara de Lobos (*see p82*). Most of these trips go only as far as Eira do Serrado, the viewing point above the village.

Village ⑩

The café owners (**above**) will urge you to try their chestnut dishes including roasted salted chestnuts, rich chestnut soup and sweet chestnut cake. Try the delicious chestnut liqueur *castanha*.

🔟⭐ Pico do Arieiro

Mountaineering equipment is not needed to get to the top of Madeira's third highest peak because a road takes you all the way from Funchal to the silence of the summit in less than an hour. The mountain top provides a viewing platform from which to look out over the peaks and ravines of the island's central mountains. From here, you have a chance to study the astonishing rock formations left over from the volcanic upheavals that created the island.

③ Sheep Pens
Livestock has been banned from the Ecological Park to allow Madeiran bilberry and heather to thrive, but sheep and goats graze around the summit and their pens can be seen.

④ West View
The view westward from the summit takes in the full central mountain range, with its succession of knife-edge peaks. The predominant colours are fiery reds, rust browns, blacks and purples of oxidized volcanic rocks, more like the surface of Mars than the Earth.

① Ice House
This igloo-shaped building **(above)**, 2 km (1 mile) south of the peak, is known as Poço da Neve ("Snow Well"), and was constructed in 1813 by an Italian ice cream maker. Ice from pits like this one provided wealthy hotel guests with so-called "snow water" in the heat of summer.

② Footpath
A footpath **(below)** links four main peaks and is one of the island's most exciting walks. It should not be attempted unless you are properly equipped for mountain conditions, including sudden storms, tunnels and unprotected drops. A large yellow sign marks the start of the path. Walk the first 100 m (328 ft) or so for fine views back to the summit.

NEED TO KNOW

MAP G4

■ There is a convenient café at the summit.

■ Pico do Arieiro can be wrapped in cloud for much of the day. Before 10am and after 5pm are best for fine weather, or take a chance during the day. It is possible to drive up through the clouds and emerge to find the peak's summit basking in sunshine.

■ Even at the height of summer, it can be very cold and windy at the summit. In winter, ice and snow are common.

8 Ecological Park

En route from Funchal, after 12 km (7 miles), you pass the entrance to the Ecological Park **(left)**, where primeval forest has been restored. With its viewing points and glades, it is a popular spot for picnics.

5 East View

The view to the east looks down over the green wooded slopes of the island's indigenous forest *(see p29)*. It is possible to see the meadows of Santo da Serra, and the island's long rocky tail.

6 Café

The photographs on the walls of the summit café show the peak at sunset, at sunrise and in snow. They might tempt you to return to enjoy the colours of the sky at dusk or dawn, or to view the night sky away from the glare of city lights.

7 Volcanic Dykes

Another distinctive feature of the view to the west and south is a series of parallel grey outcrops, resembling the Great Wall of China, that follow the contours of the landscape. These are vertical seams of hard volcanic rock that have resisted the erosive forces of rain, frost and wind.

ISLAND ORIGINS

Madeira's long, slow birth began 18 million years ago, as lava burst up through the ocean floor to create layer upon layer of basaltic rock. It took 15 million years for Pico do Arieiro to reach this height. For another 2.25 million years, further eruptions spilled lava sideways from the island's central core, creating the plains of the Paúl da Serra to the west and Santo da Serra to the east.

9 Wildlife

Even on the bare, dry rocks of Madeira's high peaks, plants find a niche wherever a crack provides shelter and moisture. Among the gorse and heather, you can spot grasshoppers and the camouflaged native grayling butterfly.

10 Trig Point

A short scramble up from the café brings you to the actual summit, 1,818 m (5,965 ft) above sea level. It is marked by a concrete post **(below)** used for measuring altitude and location.

The Top 10 of Everything

**Dancers performing during the
annual Flower Parade in Madeira**

🔟 Moments in History

1 Island Formation
Twenty million years ago, the Madeiran archipelago began to emerge from the sea (first Porto Santo, then Madeira and the Ilhas Desertas). Pockets of fertile soil were created when storms eroded the softer layers of volcanic ash.

2 Early Visitors
Sailors visited Madeira to gather sap from dragon trees for use in dying clothes. Although mentioned in the *Natural History* of Pliny the Elder (AD 23–79), Madeira was first charted on the Medici Map of 1351, appearing as "Isola de Lolegname" or the "Wooded Isle".

Henry the Navigator in his armour

3 Zarco Arrives
Prince Henry "the Navigator" (1394–1460), third son of King John I of Portugal, realized how valuable Madeira was to sailors exploring the Atlantic Ocean. He sent João Gonçalves Zarco (1387–1467) to the islands. Zarco *(see p19)* landed on Porto Santo in 1418, and returned in 1419 to claim Madeira for Portugal.

4 Colonization
Portuguese colonization of Madeira began in 1420. Machico was initially the capital, but Funchal had the better harbour and so gained city status in 1508. Upon Zarco's arrival, densely forested areas were burned to make room for farming and enslaved people were taken from Portuguese colonies to work on the land.

5 Sugar Production and Slavery
By 1470, the early settlers of Madeira were exporting wheat, dye-stuffs, wine and timber, but sugar produced the biggest profits. Trading with London, Antwerp, Venice and Genoa, the island was Europe's main sugar producer for 150 years. To meet production demands more enslaved people were brought to work in the cane fields, first from the Canary Islands and later from West Africa. Slavery persisted in Madeira until around 1773 when Marquis de Pombal abolished it.

6 Wine
Quick profits and wealth became a thing of the past once Caribbean and Brazilian sugar hit European markets in the mid-16th century. *Malvazia* (Malmsey), a rich sweet wine, took over as Madeira's main export.

7 The British Arrive
British merchants dominated the wine trade after King Charles II married the Portuguese princess Catherine of Braganza in 1662, and

Catherine of Braganza

British (and American) taxes on Madeira wine were reduced as part of the marriage settlement. So valuable was Madeira to the British, that an armed force was sent in 1801 to stop Napoleon capturing it.

8 Reid's Palace

Once the Napoleonic Wars were over, Madeira became a very popular winter holiday destination for wealthy northern Europeans. Symbolic of the era is Reid's Palace *(see p115)*, founded by William Reid, who arrived a poor sailor in 1836 and made a fortune renting houses to aristocratic visitors.

Soldiers on the streets of Lisbon

9 Autonomy

Madeira escaped the worst effects of the two World Wars, but by 1974, the year of Portugal's Carnation Revolution, it had become Europe's poorest region. In that year, Portugal's dictatorship was toppled in a coup by army officers. Later, celebrating soldiers had carnations stuck in their gun barrels by joyous civilians. In 1976, Madeira became largely autonomous, except for tax, foreign policy and defence.

10 Anniversaries

In 2008, Funchal celebrated its 500th anniversary as the capital of an increasingly prosperous island. Between 2018 and 2020, the archipelago celebrated its 600th anniversary with various events and festivities marking the discovery of the island of Porto Santo in 1418, and Madeira in 1419.

TOP 10 FAMOUS MADEIRANS

Football star Cristiano Ronaldo

1 Vicente Gomes da Silva
Silva (1827–1906) was among the earliest Portuguese photographers. His work is featured in the Madeira Photography Museum *(see p49)*.

2 Francisco Franco de Sousa
One of the top sculptors (1885–1955) of the Portuguese Modernist movement. He designed the Zarco Monument *(see p45)*.

3 Edmundo Bettencourt
A singer and a poet, Bettencourt (1899–1973) is famous for introducing new themes to Coimbra's *fado* style.

4 Martha Telles
This artist (1930–2001) started painting in Madeira as a student of Max Römer.

5 Herberto Hélder
One of the most noted Portuguese poets of the 20th century, Hélder (1930–2015) wrote experimental and surreal poems.

6 António da Cunha Telles
A pioneer of the Portuguese New Cinema movement, Cunha Telles's (b. 1935) first feature film *O Cerco* was released in 1970.

7 Paulo David
A Portuguese architect, Paulo David (b. 1959) designed the Mudas Contemporary Art Museum *(see p90)*.

8 Nini Andrade
Many hotels have had a makeover by this interior designer (b. 1962). A museum in Funchal *(see p77)* is named after her.

9 Fátima Lopes
Fashion designer Lopes (b. 1965) has her own brand shop and exhibits her collections in events around the world.

10 Cristiano Ronaldo
This famous footballer (b. 1985) from Funchal regularly returns to Madeira to visit family and friends.

🔟 Historic Buildings

1 Capela do Corpo Santo, Funchal

This 16th-century chapel situated in the Zona Velha (see pp22–3) was built and run by the Guild of São Pedro Gonçalves, a self-help charity that raised funds for fishermen and their families.

2 Capela de Santa Catarina, Funchal

MAP Q2 ■ Jardim de Santa Catarina

Founded in 1425 by Constança de Almeida, Zarco's wife, this chapel was the first to be built in Funchal.

Interior of the Fishermen's Chapel

3 Fishermen's Chapel, Câmara de Lobos

MAP F6 ■ Câmara de Lobos

This simple, moving chapel on the harbour is where fishermen come to pray before and after going to sea. Wall paintings depict the story of how St Anthony of Padua (who was born in Lisbon) survived a shipwreck, and was so eloquent that even the fishes of the sea came to hear him preach.

Câmara Municipal town square

4 Tower House, Funchal

MAP P3 ■ Rua do Bispo

Opposite the Museum of Sacred Art (see pp14–15) is a stately building with a *torre-mirante* (viewing tower). Typical of the grander of Funchal's townhouses, these towers were built for the owners to see incoming ships. Note that the door handles are made from large iron keys.

5 Capela de Santo António da Mouraria, Funchal

MAP P3 ■ Rua da Alfândega

This tiny chapel features an ornate altar with early 18th-century gilded Baroque carvings.

6 Igreja Inglesa, Funchal

MAP P2 ■ Rua do Quebra Costas

The English Church (1822) is a domed Neo-Classical building set in a delightful garden. Its construction was funded by public appeal; contributions came from Nelson, George II and the Duke of Wellington.

7 Câmara Municipal, Funchal

MAP P3 ■ Praça do Município
■ Open to the public 11am–3pm Mon–Fri ■ Adm (under 6s free)

Madeira's early 19th-century town hall originally belonged to the Count of Carvalhal (see p32). Look in the inner courtyard to see graceful balconies and a sensuous statue of *Leda and the Swan* (see p24), brought here when the market was built in 1937.

Funchal's Banco de Portugal

8 Banco de Portugal, Funchal

MAP P3 ■ Avenida Zarco

The Bank of Portugal building (1940) maintains continuity with traditional architecture, with its globe-topped corner turret, Grecian marble statues, and fruit-filled baskets symbolizing wealth and plenty. Just across the road is Francisco Franco's *Zarco Monument* (1927), showing Funchal's founder looking out to sea.

9 Alfândega, Funchal

MAP P3 ■ Avenida do Mar
■ 291 210 500 ■ By appointment

Designed in 1508 by Pêro Anes (who also designed the cathedral), the Customs House was built to collect the taxes levied by the Portuguese Crown on Madeira's timber, corn and sugar exports. Now home to the island's Regional Assembly, it has three splendid upper-floor rooms.

10 Administrative Offices, University of Madeira, Funchal

MAP P3 ■ Rua dos Ferreiros

The 17th-century buildings of what used to be the old Jesuit college have now been restored to provide new administrative offices for the University of Madeira. From the inner courtyard, there are good views of the Igreja do Colégio tower *(see p46)*.

TOP 10 FLAMBOYANT BUILDINGS IN FUNCHAL

1 Madeira Cable Car Station
This public building is a futuristic cube of steel and glass on Rua Dom Carlos.

2 New Chamber of Commerce
Today's Chamber of Commerce is located in a 15th-century building off Rua dos Aranhas.

3 Pátio
The inner courtyard of the 1860s Pátio (Rua da Carreira 43) features a sweeping double staircase leading to the Madeira Photography Museum *(see p49)*.

4 Rua da Carreira
On this street of flamboyant iron balconies, look out especially for those at numbers 77–91 and 155.

5 Rua da Mouraria
Funchal's antiques quarter has many aristocratic townhouses, including the Museu Municipal e Aquário *(see p49)*.

6 Garden Gazebo
Take tea, admire the views and watch the world go by at a *casinha de prazer* ("pleasure house") like the one in the Museu Frederico de Freitas *(see p48)*.

7 Quintas
Ornate mansions like the Quinta Palmeira and its gardens *(see p50)* line the terraces above Funchal.

8 Casino
The 1970s casino on Avenida do Infante looks wonderful lit up at night.

9 Apartamentos Navio Azul
Reminiscent of an ocean liner, this curvy 1970s block stands next to the Estrada Monumental.

10 The Ritz Restaurant
The former Chamber of Commerce on Avenida Arriaga, clad in tile pictures of Madeiran transport, now serves as an upscale restaurant.

The Ritz Restaurant, Funchal

🔟 Churches

Glorious interior of Igreja do Colégio, Funchal, filled with colourful frescoes

① Igreja do Colégio, Funchal

MAP P3 ■ Praça do Município

The Jesuits, a large brotherhood of missionary priests, owned huge wine estates on Madeira and spent some of their wealth on this lovely church, which is covered from floor to ceiling in frescoes, gilded carvings and rare ceramic tiles. The school the Jesuits built alongside the church is now the University of Madeira.

② Igreja de São Pedro, Funchal

MAP N2 ■ Rua de São Pedro

The main church until the cathedral was built, St Peter's has a wealth of gilded woodwork, some dating from the 17th century. The corn and grapes being gathered by angels in the right-hand chapel are symbolic of the bread and wine of Christ's Last Supper. A simple slab covers the grave of João de Moura Rolim (died 1661), who paid for the decoration.

③ São Salvador, Santa Cruz

MAP K5 ■ Rua Irmã Wilson

This Gothic parish church was completed in 1512, when the tomb of the merchant Micer João, supported by crouching lions, was installed on the north side. Next to it is the chapel of the Morais family (1522). The altar has 16th-century paintings depicting the life of Christ by Gregório Lopes, and the sacristy, entered through a Manueline portal, contains a 16th-century carved and painted tableau of the *Last Supper*.

④ Funchal Cathedral (Sé)

The 15th-century cathedral *(see pp12–13)* of Funchal is a blend of Portuguese, Spanish, Italian and Flemish styles. It set the pattern for the island's other churches with its beautiful *talha dourada* ("gilded woodwork"), as demonstrated in the Holy Sacrament chapel, located to the right of the high altar.

Statue, Funchal Cathedral

⑤ Igreja da Nossa Senhora da Conceição, Machico

MAP K4 ▪ Largo Dr. António Jardim d'Oliveira

Probably designed by Pêro Anes, who designed Funchal Cathedral, this church dates from 1499 and is noted for its south door – the white marble pillars come from Seville and were a gift from King Manuel I (1495–1521). The treasury displays rare and valuable 15th-century religious artifacts.

⑥ Capela dos Milagres, Machico

MAP K4 ▪ Largo Senhor dos Milagres

The Chapel of the Miracles takes its name from the 15th-century Flemish crucifix on the high altar. It was miraculously found floating at sea, years after the old chapel was washed away by a flood in 1803. The original chapel is said to have been built over the grave of Anne of Hertford and Robert Machin, legendary lovers shipwrecked here in the 14th century.

⑦ Santa Clara, Funchal

Founded in 1476 by João Gonçalves de Câmara, son of Zarco (see p19), this convent (see pp20–21) has changed very little since it was first built.

⑧ Senhora da Luz, Ponta do Sol

MAP D5 ▪ Rua Dr. João Augusto Teixeira

Founded in 1486 by Rodrigo Anes, one of the first men to be granted land on Madeira by the Portuguese king, this church has an original knotwork ceiling, a 16th-century Flemish altarpiece, as well as a ceramic font, glazed with green copper oxide to resemble bronze.

⑨ São Bento, Ribeira Brava

MAP D5 ▪ Rua Camacho 20

A lion and a basilisk (whose stare was said to turn humans to stone) are among the carvings on the capitals, font and pulpit of this Gothic parish church. Don't miss the magnificent 16th-century Flemish *Nativity* panels showing São Bento and São Bernardo and the statue of the Virgin.

Church of São Bento, Ribeira Brava

⑩ Capela do Loreto, Loreto

MAP C4 ▪ Arco da Calheta

An unspoiled, historic 16th-century church, this boasts a knotwork ceiling and Gothic doorways of imported white marble. The altar was remodelled in the 18th century.

🔟 Museums

Museu Henrique e Francisco Franco

1 Museu Henrique e Francisco Franco, Funchal

MAP N4 ■ Rua João de Deus 13 ■ 291 211 090 ■ Open 9:30am–5:30pm Mon–Fri

The Franco brothers, painter Henrique (1883–1961) and sculptor Francisco (1855–1955), left Madeira to find fame in Lisbon and Paris. Their artistic achievements are celebrated in this museum.

2 Museu da Quinta das Cruzes, Funchal

This is the house where Madeira's first ruler lived when Madeira was the newest addition to Portugal's

Casa Museu Frederico de Freitas

overseas colonies at the start of the Age of Discovery in the 15th century. Paintings and sketches of the island's major landmarks hang on the walls of the *quinta*'s richly decorated rooms (see pp18–19).

3 Museu CR7, Funchal

MAP Q2 ■ Avenida Sá Carneiro-Praça do Mar 27 ■ 291 639 880 ■ Open 10am–5pm Mon–Fri ■ Adm ■ www.museucr7.com

A must for all football fans, especially any enamoured by Cristiano Ronaldo and his number 7 shirt. The museum (see p59) showcases trophies and medals awarded to the Madeira-born, Portuguese international star.

4 Museu de Arte Sacra, Funchal

Funchal's Religious Art Museum (see pp14–15) is known for its colourful 16th-century Flemish paintings, but also contains many remarkable polychrome wooden statues.

5 Casa Museu Frederico de Freitas, Funchal

MAP P2 ■ Calçada de Santa Clara 7 ■ 291 202 570 ■ Open 10am–5:30pm Tue–Sat ■ Adm

Packed with antiques and religious paintings, this museum also has an amusing collection of teapots from all over the world. A wing is devoted to ceramic tiles, with early examples from long-gone Madeiran churches.

6 Museu a Cidade do Açúcar, Funchal

MAP P3 ■ Praça Colombo 5 ■ 291 211 037 ■ Open 9:30am–5:30pm Mon–Fri

Funchal's history is chronicled in fascinating detail by exploring its once-thriving sugar cane industry.

7 Núcleo Museológico do Bordado

MAP N4 ■ Rua do Visconde do Anadia 44 ■ 291 211 600 ■ Open 9:30am–12:30pm & 2–5:30pm Mon–Fri ■ Adm ■ www.bordadomadeira.com

The exhibits showcase the history of Madeira's embroidery, tapestry, handicrafts and colourful costumes.

Blue whale model at Museu da Baleia

8 Museu da Baleia, Caniçal

MAP L4 ■ Rua da Pedra d'Eira ■ 291 961 858 ■ Open 11am–6pm Tue–Sun ■ Adm ■ www.museudabaleia.org

Madeira's Whale Museum depicts the evolution of dolphins and whales with interactive and 3D displays. Exhibits include a whaling boat.

9 Madeira Story Centre, Funchal

This interactive museum covers all aspects of the island's history (see p23). There's also a rooftop restaurant and a shop selling crafts.

10 Madeira Photography Museum, Funchal

MAP P2 ■ Rua da Carreira 43 ■ 291 145 325 ■ Open 10am–7pm Tue–Sat ■ Adm

In addition to paying tribute to Vicente Gomes da Silva, a Portuguese photography pioneer, this museum serves as a visual reference to Madeira's photographic heritage over the last 150 years.

TOP 10 MUSEUM EXHIBITS

Sculptures, Monte Palace Museum

1 Wood Sculpture
Rare tribal sculpture from Zimbabwe dating from the 1950s and 1960s can be seen at the museum in Monte Tropical Palace Garden (see p34).

2 Football Trophies
Cristiano Ronaldo's impressive awards, including the Ballon d'Or and Golden Shoe, are displayed in a suitably dazzling fashion at Museu CR7.

3 Indian Miniature
In this exquisite painting at Museu da Quinta das Cruzes (see pp18–19), the Virgin is depicted as a Mogul princess.

4 Processional Cross
View Renaissance silverwork, with the Evangelists and biblical scenes in relief, at Museu de Arte Sacra (see p14).

5 City Coat of Arms
Museu a Cidade do Açúcar houses an unusual example from 1584 depicting elements of sugar cane iconography.

6 Moray Eels
Sharp-fanged denizens of the deep can be admired at Museu Municipal e Aquário.

7 Winter Garden
Casa Museu Frederico de Freitas features a fern-filled, Art Nouveau conservatory.

8 Boy with Cockerel
Housed in Museu Henrique e Francisco Franco, this portrait of a peasant boy is one of Henrique Franco's best.

9 Portraits of Columbus
Paintings and drawings of Christopher Columbus line the walls of Casa Museu Cristóvão Colombo (see p102).

10 Scrimshaws
Museu da Baleia exhibits whalebones carved and etched in the days before hunting whales was illegal.

ᵀᴼᴾ**10** Gardens

1 Monte Palace Tropical Garden, Monte

This intriguing botanical garden *(see p34)* has caves, fountains, lakes, fish ponds, Japanese temples, sculptures, novel tile pictures as well as a museum.

Statue in Monte Palace Tropical Garden

2 Santa Catarina Park, Funchal

MAP Q2 ▪ Avenida do Infante

Located on the way from downtown Funchal to the Hotel Zone, this terraced park has fantastic views over the harbour. The big lake at the centre is home to swans and ducks and there's also a children's playground. Look out for the Capela de Santa Catarina *(see p44)* and the old machinery on display which was once used to crush grapes and lay asphalt.

3 Quinta das Cruzes, Funchal

The flower-filled grounds of this "archaeological park" *(see pp18–19)* boasts grave slabs, a private chapel, a wonderful orchid garden *(see p18)* and a *casinha de prazer* ("pleasure house"), perched on the walls to take advantage of the views.

Display of flowers, Jardim Botânico

4 Ribeiro Frio Forest Park

MAP H4 ▪ São Roque do Faial ▪ 291 575 434

The park comprises a wide area of the UNESCO-listed *laurissilva* forest. Hikers will find several fantastic mountain walks here, such as the Levada do Furado *(see p55)*. For others, the village has a trout farm to visit and a rustic restaurant *(see p83)* to enjoy.

5 Quinta Palmeira, Funchal

MAP G6 ▪ Rua da Levada de Santa Luzia 31A ▪ 291 221 091 ▪ Closed for renovation ▪ Adm

Despite being blighted by its proximity to one of Funchal's fast highways, this former home of the Gordon wine family hovers between garden and wilderness, with manicured rose gardens, tiled fountains, grottoes and some jungle-like areas. Don't miss the 15th-century Columbus Window, rescued from the home of João Esmeraldo.

6 Jardim Botânico, Funchal

These extraordinary gardens *(see pp26–9)* are a showcase for Madeira's varied plant life.

Jardins Quinta da Boa Vista

Visit this wonderfully appealing subtropical garden complex *(see p64)* between December and May to witness the orchid collection in all its exquisite finery. The rest of the estate is dedicated to re-creating the habitats of endangered plant species.

Quinta Vigia, Funchal

MAP Q1 ■ Avenida do Infante
The well-kept gardens of Madeira's president are open on weekdays, so long as there are no official functions.

Fountain in Quinta Vigia, Funchal

Quinta do Palheiro Ferreiro

Situated in an enviable location above Funchal, unusual and imaginative subtropical plants are displayed at this estate *(see pp32–3)* in a style that is recognizably English.

Jardim de São Francisco, Funchal

MAP P2 ■ Avenida Arriaga
St Francis, the patron saint of the environment, would firmly approve of this richly planted garden, built in the city centre on the site of Funchal's long-gone Franciscan friary. It is only the size of a city block, but so full of scented and flowering plants, shaded by some truly enormous trees, that you could be in the middle of the jungle.

TOP 10 MADEIRAN PLANTS AND FLOWERS

Beautiful king protea plants

1 King Protea
These South African plants, similar to giant artichokes, are in demand for flower displays.

2 Slipper Orchid
Mainly flowering in the winter months, slipper orchids need jungle-like shade.

3 Mexican Poinsettia
These festive plants bloom right on cue for Christmas; note that the showy, scarlet part is actually the bract, not the flower.

4 Aloe
Fleshy leaves edged with spines produce flower spikes up to 1 m (3 ft) high. The sap is harvested, and used in making aloe vera skin products.

5 Agapanthus
The blue-and-white globe-shaped blossoms of the Lily of the Nile line Madeira's roadside banks in summer.

6 Strelitzia
Is it a bird or is it a plant? These long-lived flowers look like exotic birds of paradise.

7 Angel's Trumpet
White, yellow or amber, the datura's long trumpets smell and look lovely.

8 Arum Lily
Pure white and sweetly scented, these flowers symbolize the Virgin Mary and virginity.

9 Flame of the Forest
Crowned by orange-red coxcombs, these trees are descended from the seeds brought to Madeira by Captain Cook in 1772.

10 Jacaranda
Funchal's Avenida Arriaga turns into a river of blue when these striking Brazilian trees flower in spring.

Top 10 Beaches

Glorious, wide stretch of golden sand at Porto Santo

1 Porto Santo
MAP L2

Travel 40 km (25 miles) northeast of Madeira to enjoy the vast stretch of unspoilt golden sand of Porto Santo (see p102). The Fontinha section offers ramps, toilets and amphibian-use wheelchairs.

2 Calheta
MAP B4

With golden sand specially imported from Morocco, this artificial beach is protected by two breakwaters and is popular, getting crowded during the summer. There are watersports facilities here – this is a great launch pad for canoeists and windsurfers.

3 Prainha
MAP L4

A pretty, sheltered bay with a café at its eastern end, pocket-sized Prainha ("Little Beach") has one of Madeira's naturally sandy beaches.

Prainha's sand beach

4 São Tiago
MAP Q6

A small pebble beach sited under the shadow of Fortaleza de São Tiago (see p22), this is a popular summer destination for locals. A promenade set alongside the fortress walls has extra sunbathing spots. Natural rock formations add to the allure of the beach with its warm shallow water. There are freshwater showers.

5 Praia Formosa
MAP G6

Steep-sided Madeira does not have many beaches – cliffs and rocky shores are the norm – but this, the "Beautiful Beach", is a stretch of grey, sea-smoothed pebbles situated between Funchal and Câmara de Lobos. There are changing facilities, a lifeguard post and also a children's playground at the location.

6 Machico
MAP K4

Positioned near the original basalt pebble beach is the town's artificial alternative, made with sand imported from the Western Sahara in North Africa. The luxuriously soft beach, known as Banda d'Além, is 125 m (410 ft) in length and 70 m (230 ft) wide. It is popular with locals as well as tourists, especially at weekends.

7 Ponta do Sol
MAP D5

The beach at Ponta do Sol ("Sun Point") is the perfect place to watch the setting sun. Dramatic clouds float like islands in a sky coloured pink and purple.

8 Garajau and Caniço
MAP J6

A path from the statue of Christ the Redeemer at Garajau winds down to a beach popular for snorkelling and diving. It marks the start of a marine reserve with underwater caves leading to Caniço de Baixo *(see p57)*.

9 Praia dos Reis Magos
MAP J6

Continuing eastwards from Caniço de Baixo, a seafront promenade leads to Praia dos Reis Magos, a rocky beach with a scattering of fishermen's huts as well as a couple of simple cafés selling freshly grilled fish. This is an idyllic spot for romantics who prefer to be away from the crowds.

Beach and rock pools near São Jorge

10 São Jorge
MAP H2

About 2 km (1 mile) east of São Jorge, a sign to *praia* ("beach") leads to the estuary of the São Jorge river, where you can swim in a natural pool or in the sea (access via the small pebbled beach). There's a simple beach café.

TOP 10 NATURAL SWIMMING POOLS AND BATHING COMPLEXES

Natural rock pools, Porto Moniz

1 Porto Moniz
MAP C1 ▪ Adm
Natural rock pools famous across the island. Lockers plus summer snack bar.

2 Reid's Palace
MAP G6 ▪ Adm
Three luxurious pools, shaded by palms in a garden setting *(see p115)*.

3 Ponta Delgada
MAP F2 ▪ Adm
Two seawater bathing pools, with shower facilities and other amenities.

4 Ponta Gorda
MAP G6 ▪ Adm
Kids can play in the adventure pools, while adults can sunbathe seaside.

5 Porto da Cruz
MAP J3 ▪ Adm
Sun loungers and umbrellas around two swimming pools on the rocky coastline.

6 Seixal
MAP D2
Close to Laje Beach, natural pools in a lovely landscape with very clear water.

7 Ribeira Brava
MAP D5
A pebble and black sand beach with a pool facility, which has changing rooms, toilets and restaurant.

8 Barreirinha
MAP Q5 ▪ Adm
Pool and sunbathing area at São Tiago Beach, with lockers, toilets and a bar.

9 Calhau de São Jorge
MAP H2 ▪ Adm
Located near Santana, this pool complex provides a safe swimming haven next to an often-rough sea.

10 Doca do Cavacas
MAP G6 ▪ Adm
Natural volcanic pools enclosed by sculpted rock peer out over open sea. Access via Funchal's Lido promenade.

TOP 10 Levada Walks and Hiking Trails

Cliffs of Ponta de São Lourenço

1 Ponta de São Lourenço
MAP M4

The easternmost peninsula on the island, Ponta de São Lourenço (see p94) makes for a bracing there-and-back coastal amble over undulating, often vertiginous landscape. Starting at the Baía d'Abra car park, the trail follows the peninsula's pointed finger and gives impressive Atlantic views. There is little shade, and strong gusts are commonplace.

2 Pico do Arieiro–Pico Ruivo
MAP G4

This challenging mountain hike connects Madeira's third-highest peak, Pico do Arieiro (see pp38–9) with the highest, Pico Ruivo. You'll also scale the second-highest, Pico das Torres. Take warm clothing, plenty of water and a torch for the tunnels. A guide is recommended or climb as part of an organized hike.

Along the Pico do Arieiro

3 Vereda do Fanal
MAP C2

Commencing from the ER209 road on the Paúl da Serra plateau (see p89), this trail meanders through the pristine *laurissilva* forest (see p29) and crosses Fanal, a scenic volcanic crater set within the Madeira Natural Park. Hikers should take care as there can be frequent patches of fog along the trail.

4 Prazeres–Paúl do Mar
MAP B3

A bracing coastal jaunt that begins in Prazeres (see p90), the path corkscrews down to the sea and skirts a lovely waterfall, with panoramic views across Madeira's southwest region.

5 Santana–São Jorge–Vigia
MAP H2

From Santana there is an occasionally precipitous route that snakes above a restless sea. The track passes Quinta do Furão (see p85) and edges up a narrow path before descending to São Jorge. From here it's a scenic stroll to the lighthouse crowning Vigia.

6 Levada do Moinho
MAP A2

Beginning at Ribeira da Cruz on the ER101 just south of Ponta do Pargo (see p88), this charming walk is named after *moinhos* (water mills) that used to line the route, the ruins of which can still be admired. The trail ends in Junqueira, near Porto Moniz (see p88).

7 Boca da Corrida–Encumeada
MAP G4

Called Caminho Real da Encumeada ("Royal Road"), this trail crosses part of Madeira's central massif and runs along the foot of some of the island's highest peaks. Boca da Corrida marks the start, below which is Curral das Freiras *(see pp36–7)*.

8 Rabaçal–Levada do Risco–Levada das 25 Fontes
MAP C3

A tumbling waterfall near Rabaçal *(see p87)* marks the start of these *levada* walks. Bubbling springs, crystal clear pools and lagoons also appeal. Take care at the Ribeira Grande.

Hiking to Caldeirão Verde

9 Queimadas–Levada do Caldeirão Verde–Santana
MAP H3

The trail that winds the walkways of this scenic *levada* leads to the verdant Queimadas but it also takes in spectacular ravines, cascading waterfalls and four moss-textured tunnels – don't forget to bring a torch!

10 Levada do Furado
MAP H4

One of the oldest *levadas* starts at Ribeiro Frio *(see p83)*, 860 m (2,820 ft) above sea level. A watercourse snakes through paths in the rock, then descends to the village of Portela.

TOP 10 COAST AND MOUNTAIN VIEWPOINTS

1 Pico do Arieiro
MAP G4
The summit of the third-highest peak on the island can be reached by road.

2 Cabo Girão
MAP E5
A glass floor adds to the giddy view over one of Europe's tallest sea cliffs.

3 Morro do Furado
MAP M4
On a clear day you can see Porto Santo Island from this lofty standpoint at the end of Ponta de São Lourenço.

4 Boca da Corrida
MAP F4
Magnificent mountain vistas including Curral das Freiras can be admired from this popular viewpoint.

5 Portela
MAP J4
Panoramas from Miradouro da Portela embrace Penha de Águia *(see p84)*.

6 Balcões
MAP H4
Hikers enjoy views of the Ribeira da Metade Valley, near Ribeiro Frio *(see p83)*.

7 Cabanas
MAP G2
Between São Jorge *(see p84)* and Arco de São Jorge, the view is laced with salt.

8 Bica da Cana
MAP E3
Marked with a cairn, the outlook here takes in high peaks and drifting cloud.

9 Rabaçal
MAP C3
Head for Pico da Urze, in Paúl da Serra, for valley views and *laurissilva* forest.

10 Eira do Serrado
MAP F4
A footpath from the Eira do Serrado hotel *(see p116)* offers a mountain panorama.

Eira do Serrado viewpoint

🔟 Outdoor Activities

1 Bird-Watching
Madeira Wind Birds: MAP H5; 917 777 441; www.madeirawindbirds.com (for expeditions)

The Madeira archipelago offers excellent opportunities for birders. The islands are home to 42 breeding species, three of which are endemic to Madeira: these are the Zino's petrel, the Trocaz pigeon and the Madeira firecrest. Seabirds are prevalent, while Berthelot's pipit is always a prized sighting.

2 Windsurfing
Mar Dourado: MAP L2; 963 970 789

For the most part fanned by gentle sea breezes, the shallow, remarkably clear water lapping at Porto Santo beach (see p102) is perfectly suited to windsurfing. Mar Dourado, located on the expansive sands below the Torre Praia Hotel, offers expert windsurfing. Board and equipment hire is also available. The company also organizes a range of other watersports (see p104) activities.

Windsurfing in Funchal harbour

Mountain biking on a rocky slope

3 Mountain Biking
Free Ride: MAP G6; 925 977 046; www.freeridemadeira.com

The island's rugged terrain presents challenging tracks as well as gravity-defying inclines. Following *levada (see pp54–5)* footpaths is an easier option. Rent or join an organized excursion.

4 Horse Riding
Quinta do Riacho: MAP J4; 967 010 015; www.quintadoriacho.com ▪ Escapada dos Cavaleiros: MAP F5; 966 312 151; www.escapadados cavaleiros.com

Several companies in Madeira offer horse riding activities, lessons and guided tours along mountain tracks and forest byways. There are similar options on Porto Santo (see p104).

5 Adventure Sports
True Spirit Madeira: MAP G6; 918 828 801; www.adventure madeira.com ▪ Lokoloko: MAP J6; 969 570 780; www.lokoloko madeira.com

Madeira's countryside offers plenty of adventure sports, from trekking and rock climbing to hang gliding and orienteering. Companies such as True Spirit and Lokoloko provide organized excursions.

6 Walking
With more than 1,600 km (994 miles) of footpaths, it's no wonder that thousands of people visit to walk in the island's mountains and forests.

(7) Boat Trips

Madeira Boat Trips: MAP Q3; Funchal Marina; 969 351 568/ 918 375 661 ■ Bonita da Madeira: MAP Q3; Funchal Marina; 291 762 218 Booths located around Funchal's marina have details of all the cruising options available, from day-long trips to the Ilhas Desertas (see p95) to shorter sunset cruises around the island.

(8) Deep-Sea Fishing

Balancal: MAP Q3; Funchal Marina; 291 790 350 ■ Nautisantos: MAP Q3; Funchal Marina; 291 231 312 Fishing trips can be booked at the marina. A tag-and-release policy means fish are released back into the ocean.

(9) Golf

Clube de Golfe de Santo da Serra: MAP K4; 291 550 100 ■ Palheiro Golf: MAP J5; Sítio do Balancal, São Gonçalo; 291 790 120 Two of Europe's most scenic courses are located in the east of the island at Santo da Serra and Palheiro Ferreira. Transport can be arranged from Funchal, and equipment hired.

Scuba diver watching a school of fish

(10) Diving

Manta Diving Center: MAP J6; Hotel Galomar, Caniço de Baixo; 291 935 588 ■ Madeira Divepoint: MAP H6; Pestana Carlton Madeira Hotel, Largo António Nobre, Funchal; 291 239 579 Clean Atlantic waters with an array of beautiful fish and reefs have made Madeira a popular spot for divers of all ages and all abilities.

TOP 10 MADEIRAN WILDLIFE

Red-breasted robin

1 Robins
The robins you will see on Madeira have a reddish orange breast and face.

2 Madeira Pipistrelle Bat
Endemic to Madeira, the Azores and the Canary Islands, this is a rare and critically endangered species.

3 Wagtails
This yellow-breasted bird is never very far from water, hence its Madeiran nickname: "the washerwoman".

4 Zino's Petrel
One of Europe's most endangered seabirds, Zino's Petrel only breeds on the island of Madeira.

5 Trocaz Pigeon
This shy, endemic species makes its home in the island's dense *laurissilva* forest (see p29).

6 Madeira Firecrest
These small birds, with orange or yellow crown stripes, are commonly seen in mixed woodland and gardens.

7 Sally Lightfoot Crabs
These dark brown crabs are often seen grazing tidal rocks for algae. They will disappear fast if threatened – hence their "lightfoot" name.

8 Perez's Frogs
Introduced to Madeira by the Count of Carvalhal, this noisy frog with a bright yellow backbone stripe has spread to every pond in the island.

9 Monarch Butterflies
These large orange-black-and-white gliding butterflies are seen in all Madeiran gardens.

10 Limpets
Limpets are a traditional food on Madeira, but harvesting is controlled to prevent over-exploitation.

TOP 10 Children's Attractions

① Grutas de São Vicente
MAP E2 ▪ São Vicente, Sítio do Pé do Passo ▪ 291 842 404 ▪ Open 10am–6pm daily ▪ Adm ▪ www.grutasecentrodovulcanismosaovicente.com

These caves were created by molten rock. A cave tour, simulated eruptions and a short film teaches both children and adults about the volcanic origins of Madeira.

Volcanic caves at São Vicente

② Madeira Theme Park
MAP H2 ▪ Estrada do Parque Temático 1, Fonte da Pedra, Santana ▪ 291 570 410 ▪ Open 10am–7pm daily (Oct–Mar: 9am–6pm daily) ▪ Adm ▪ www.parquetematicodamadeira.pt

Set around a boating lake, the park boasts a number of pavilions devoted to the island's heritage and traditions. There's a maze to get lost in and a radical sports zone to check out. Children also have their own playground.

③ Santa Catarina Park
Offering a very attractive view out over Funchal Bay, these beautiful public gardens (see p50) also feature a children's playground and a palm-fringed lake where youngsters will enjoy feeding the resident swans and ducks while adults take a pause.

④ Dolphin-Watching
MAP Q3 ▪ Tickets from Marina do Funchal ▪ 291 231 312 ▪ Adm

Few encounters with nature are as exciting as those with dolphins or whales in their natural habitat, but this trip will appeal more to older children, because a patient wait does not always mean the animals will make an appearance.

⑤ Aquaparque
MAP K5 ▪ Ribeira da Boavista, Santa Cruz ▪ 291 524 412 ▪ Open Jun–Oct: 10am–6pm daily (till 7pm Aug) ▪ Adm

This landscaped water park features twisting slides, rapids and waterfalls. The Infant Zone's shallow pool and "lazy river" is ideal for toddlers.

⑥ Santa Maria de Colombo
MAP Q3 ▪ Tickets from Marina do Funchal ▪ 291 220 327 ▪ Trips 10:30am–1:30pm & 3–6pm daily ▪ Adm ▪ www.santamariadecolombo.com

There are many boat trips to choose from (see p57), but children will particularly enjoy a trip on a replica of the Santa Maria, the ship that took Christopher Columbus across the Atlantic on his first voyage from Europe to the Americas.

Cruising on the Santa Maria

Cable Car from Funchal to Monte

(7) Monte Cable Car

The Monte *teleférico* or cable car *(see p34)* flies spectacularly high over the João Gomes Valley, with children under six travelling for free. Once in Monte, you can explore the Palace Tropical Garden *(see p34)*.

(8) Museu CR7

Young football fans can pay homage to Cristiano Ronaldo at this museum dedicated to one of the biggest names in the sport. The footballer's statue in front of the museum *(see p48)* provides a great selfie opportunity.

(9) 3D Fun Art

MAP P2 ■ Rua do Surdo 24 ■ 291 224 745 ■ Open 10am–6pm Tue–Sun ■ Adm ■ www.3dfunart.com

Fancy being eaten by a shark? Or walking through an upside down room? Things are not what they seem at this family-friendly attraction, where the magic of optical illusion makes anything possible.

(10) Living Science Centre

MAP B1 ■ Rotunda do Ilhéu Mole ■ 291 854 274 ■ Open 10am–6pm daily ■ Adm ■ www.porto moniz.pt

This cultural centre has engaging interactive exhibitions. Look out for the 3D film about the UNESCO-designated *laurissilva* forest *(see p29)*.

TOP 10 TIPS FOR FAMILIES

1 Watersports
Whether it's riding a kayak through sea caves or joining a surf class, the island provides many family-friendly activities.

2 Indulgence
Madeirans love children, so yours will get plenty of friendly attention.

3 Downtown
You can safely let older children wander on their own; crime is almost nonexistent on the island.

4 Lido Cinemas
MAP G6 ■ 291 706 800
The Forum Madeira mall *(see p77)* has a multiplex cinema. Foreign films, except animated features, are subtitled.

5 History Lesson
Learn about the island at the Madeira Story Centre *(see p23)*, which has engaging historical and cultural displays for both adults and children.

6 Playgrounds
The best playgrounds in Funchal are in the grounds of Quinta Magnólia and Jardim de Santa Catarina *(see p50)*.

7 Funchal Marina
MAP Q3
Stroll around the marina to spot fish, boats and pictures painted on the concrete walls by visiting sailors.

8 Promenade
Many families stroll along Avenida do Mar and buy snacks from the kiosks.

9 Porto Santo
Virtually traffic free, Porto Santo is a place to let your children off the leash to explore by bike or on foot.

10 Porto Moniz
MAP B1
Known as "nature's pools", the rock pools at Porto Moniz are great for bathing in warm, shallow water.

Rock pools at Porto Moniz

TOP 10 Restaurants

Classy interior of the exclusive, Michelin-starred Il Gallo d'Oro

1 Il Gallo d'Oro

Chef Benoît Sinthon's vision and technique has won this exclusive gourmet restaurant *(see p79)* two Michelin stars. Besides an à la carte choice, diners can opt for the Signature Menu, a gastronomic treat using local and Mediterranean flavours complemented by memorable wines. Reservations essential.

2 William

Housed in the world-famous Reid's, William's *(see p79)* has elegant waiting staff serving one-star Michelin cuisine under crystal chandeliers. The dress code is smart formal: gentlemen need a jacket. Book ahead as it gets busy.

3 Gavião Novo

A restaurant celebrated for its exceptional (locally caught) fish and seafood menu, Gavião Novo *(see p79)* offers authentic dining in the heart of the Zona Velha. Visitors can mix with locals who are drawn to a menu that features island favourites such as *espetada* – skewers filled with meats and poultry. The fish dishes are also excellent.

4 Dona Amelia

A long-established restaurant, Dona Amelia has a favourable reputation. The chef's suggestions at this cheery eatery include delicious seafood risotto and succulent steak tartare. Dessert choices list crêpes flambés. Island and mainland wines are available and a cocktail bar for aperitifs.

5 Vila do Peixe

Diners get a wonderful view to write home about as they sample some of the tastiest fish and seafood found in this part of the island. Try the market fish platter, slow-grilled to perfection over glowing embers. Smart and chic, this venue *(see p85)* is a favourite with groups so check availability well ahead.

6 La Perla

The charming 19th-century manor house Quinta Splendida houses this noted gourmet hot spot *(see p99)*. Honoured by culinary awards, La Perla prides itself on its seasonal menu of regional and southern European dishes prepared with panache.

7 Abrigo do Pastor

The rustic decor sets the theme for this atmospheric eatery *(see p99)*. The food is rich and hearty: *javali* (wild boar) is always on the menu. Plates of rabbit or goat stew also feature. On Sundays they serve a special, *cozido à Portuguesa* – a grand concoction of meats, potato and vegetables.

8 Tasca Literária Dona Joana Rabo-de-Peixe

A quirky decor of photographs of local writers and books adds character to this delightful eatery *(see p79)*. This is where the Art of Open Doors project *(see p22)* began, over small plates of *petiscos* (snacks) and wine.

9 Cantinho da Serra

Eat here in winter and be treated to a roaring log fire at this country inn *(see p85)* where the menu celebrates tasty Portuguese cuisine made from traditional recipes. Food is served in clay pots, lending a rustic, authentic flavour to the proceedings.

10 Quinta do Furão

Known for its modern take on typical Madeiran gastronomy, this hotel-restaurant *(see p85)* also has a vegetarian menu. The wine list links Portuguese labels with your meal. Ask for a table on the terrace, with wonderful views.

Terrace tables at Quinta do Furão

TOP 10 MADEIRAN DISHES

Fish soup with tomato

1 Sopa de Tomate e Cebola
Tomato and onion soup crowned with a boiled egg and garnished with chopped parsley.

2 Açorda
Soup flavoured with garlic and coriander, made with bread and golden olive oil, topped off with a poached egg.

3 Espetada
Herb-flavoured barbecued beef, sometimes served on skewers that hang from a frame by your table.

4 Milho Frito
Deep-fried maize (like Italian polenta), traditionally served with *espetada*, though fries are now more common.

5 Lapas
Limpets, plucked from Madeira's rocky shores and grilled with garlic butter.

6 Bolo do Caco
Madeiran leavened flat-bread, baked on top of the oven and served plain or with garlic and herb butter.

7 Espada
Scabbard fish, a succulent and (usually) boneless white fish, traditionally served grilled with fried banana.

8 Prego
Delicious Madeiran fast food – grilled steak in a bread bun (*prego special* has ham and/or cheese as well).

9 Picado
Succulent pieces of beef, fried with garlic and red peppers, served up with French fries.

10 Bacalhau
Dried salted cod – very traditional, but an acquired taste, served in many ways, including with potatoes and egg, or casseroled with tomatoes and onion.

🔟 Wine Outlets

1 Blandy's Wine Lodge, Funchal

Set in a 17th-century friary, this lodge (see pp16–17) offers tastings and tours. Take a Vintage Tour for in-depth information.

2 Justino's, Funchal

MAP L4 ■ Parque Industrial da Cancela, Caniço ■ 291 934 257 ■ www.justinosmadeira.com

Established in 1870, Justino's is one of the island's oldest producers of Madeira wine. Its modern premises stock award-winning labels. Private visits can be arranged by appointment; call ahead.

3 H M Borges, Funchal

MAP N3 ■ Rua 31 de Janeiro ■ 291 223 247 ■ www.hmborges.com

Founded in 1877, this family-run company sells blended as well as harvest wines, along with a selection of special Frasqueira vintage wines. There is also a convivial 19th-century tasting room where visitors can sample the wines.

4 Pérola dos Vinhos

MAP P3 ■ Rua da Alfândega 119 ■ 291 644 919 ■ Closed Sun ■ www.peroladosvinhos.com

This small shop offers a wide range of Portuguese regional wines,

including wines from Madeira. Ask about the "Pérola Wine on-board", which is a boat trip combining wine tasting with fresh sushi.

Blandy's Madeira wine

5 Loja dos Vinhos, Funchal

MAP G6 ■ Estrada Monumental 314A ■ 291 761 508

Located in the hotel district, and open late, this wine shop sells the vintages of all of Madeira's main producers, including some rare bottles from the 19th century. They will also take telephone orders and make hotel deliveries.

6 J Faria & Filhos, Funchal

MAP G5 ■ Travessa do Tanque 85 ■ 291 742 935

One of several producers included on the Madeira Wine Route who have opened their doors to visitors, J Faria & Filhos is known for its splendid 10-year-old Bual. Interestingly, they also produce rum here.

7 D'Oliveiras, Funchal

MAP N3 ■ Rua dos Ferreiros 107 ■ 291 220 784

Set in a timber barn with a carved stone door, this wine lodge offers vintages from 1850, younger wines, miniatures and gift boxes.

Cosy interior of D'Oliveiras

⑧ Henriques & Henriques, Câmara de Lobos

MAP F6 ■ Avenida da Autonomia 10 ■ 291 941 551 ■ www.henriquese henriques.pt

Founded in 1850, this firm has won a string of medals and awards for dispelling the fusty image of Madeira wine and winning back a younger clientele. They introduced stylish modern labels and bottle designs, while retaining the traditional qualities of the wines themselves.

⑨ Vinhos Barbeito, Câmara de Lobos

MAP F6 ■ Estrada da Ribeira Gracia, Parque Empresarial de Câmara de Lobos ■ 291 761 829 ■ www. vinhosbarbeito.com

This revered Madeira wine label ages its wines in giant, iron-hooped barrels made from American oak and satinwood. Their wines include 3-, 5-, 10- and special 20-year-old bottles and Reserves.

Vineyards at Quinta do Furão

⑩ Quinta do Furão, Santana

MAP H2 ■ Estada Quinta do Furão 6, Santana ■ 291 570 100 ■ www. quintadofurao.com

This hotel, restaurant and wine shop (see p85) belonging to the Madeira Wine Company is set amid extensive vineyards near Santana, in the north of the island. Visitors can follow lovely trails through the vineyards, and help with the harvest during late summer and early autumn. In the wine cellar you can taste and buy four types of Madeira wine.

TOP 10 MADEIRAN WINE TERMS

Bottles of Madeira wine

1 Sercial
The driest of the traditional Madeira wines. Excellent aperitif or with soup.

2 Verdelho
A tawny, medium dry wine good for drinking with food.

3 Bual/Boal
A nutty dessert wine ideal with cheese or puddings.

4 Malmsey/Malvasia
The richest and sweetest Madeira wine, best for after-dinner drinking.

5 Dry, Medium Dry and Medium Sweet
These wines are three years old, and made from *tinta negra mole* grapes. They lack the depth of real Madeira.

6 Estufagem
The process of ageing the wine in casks kept in an *estufa* (hothouse), or of heating the wine in tanks to make it age even faster. The second method yields inferior results.

7 Canteiro
The term *canteiro* is used to distinguish quality wines and is a slow method of ageing Madeira in casks heated naturally by the sun.

8 Reserve
A blend of wines made by the two methods of *estufagem* and with an average age of five years. Made mostly with *tinta negra mole* grapes.

9 Special Reserve
A blend of wines aged in casks for about ten years. They are usually made with the noble grape varieties (1–4 above).

10 Vintage Wines
The finest Madeira, aged for a minimum of 20 years in casks and a further two years in the bottle.

🔟 Specialist Shops

1 Jardins Quinta da Boa Vista, Funchal

MAP H5 ■ Rua do Lombo da Boa Vista 25 ■ 291 220 468 ■ Open 9am–5:30pm Mon–Sat ■ Adm

Boa Vista *(see p51)* specialize in brightly coloured *bromeliads* ("air plants"), but also grow and sell a great range of other exotic plants.

Orchids growing at Boa Vista Orchids

2 Armazém do Mercado, Funchal

The "Warehouse Market" *(see p23)* is filled with pop-up boutiques selling products that are ideal for gifts or souvenirs, from trinkets to locally produced wine and various foodstuffs.

3 Fábrica de Chapéus de Santa Maria, Funchal

MAP P5 ■ Rua de Santa Maria 237 ■ 291 223 814

This local workshop offers the island's iconic hats. On display are the chapéus de Carreiro, straw hats worn by the toboggan drivers *(see p34)*. Look out for the *carapuças* (a pointy woollen cap) that was traditionally worn by Madeirans, and is now a great souvenir.

4 Bordal, Funchal

MAP P4 ■ Rua Dr. Fernão Ornelas 77 ■ 291 222 965 ■ www.bordal.pt

Founded in 1962, Bordal specializes in handmade embroidery pieces, including small handkerchiefs, baby clothes and quilts. The in-house factory has a replica of the layette made for the first daughter of the Duke of York.

5 Patricio & Gouveia, Funchal

MAP P4 ■ Rua Visconde de Anadia 34 ■ 291 220 801

Tour the embroidery factory to find out how traditional designs are transferred from parchment to linen, before browsing the shop for blouses, tablecloths and night-gowns with beautiful antique lace.

6 A Confeitaria, Funchal

MAP Q1 ■ Avenida do Infante, Edifício Quinta Vitória 28 ■ 291 621 325

A decadent assortment of delicious artisan cakes and pastries, plus traditional favourites including *bolo de mel* (honey cake) are sold at this busy bakery, where the motto is "bake the world a better place".

7 Fábrica Santo António, Funchal

MAP P4 ■ Travessa do Forno 27–9 ■ 291 220 255 ■ www.fabricasto antonio.com

One of the most iconic stores in Funchal, Fábrica Santo António is the place to go for homemade can-dies, cookies and jams. The period furnishings in the store lend the place an authentic yesteryear charm.

Tasty treats at Fábrica Santo António

Books at Livraria Esperança

⑧ Livraria Esperança, Funchal

Even if you can't read Portuguese, Livraria Esperança (see p77) is well worth a visit. Filling an old palace, Portugal's biggest bookstore is charmingly old-fashioned. There are volumes on every theme possible here, from children's books to brain-surgery manuals. Alongside these are a few titles in English.

⑨ Casa do Turista, Funchal

MAP P2 ■ Galerias São Lourenço 24 ■ 291 200 600 ■ Open 10am–7pm Mon–Sat

Housed in the Galerias São Lourenço, this "Tourist House" (see p77) boasts a wide range of Portuguese-made silver, ceramics, glassware and linen.

⑩ Loja Jacarandá, Funchal

MAP P3 ■ Rua da Sé 30 ■ 291 231 235

A few steps away from the Funchal Cathedral (see p46), this delightful shop stands out with its black tile façade. Inside you'll find a series of cork items, including bags and shoes. The shop also features a food section that offers local Madeiran produce, such as jams, honey cake and wine.

TOP 10 GIFTS TO BUY

1 Pompom Hats
Thick, cable-knit hats and sweaters made from raw undyed wool are worn by Madeira's farmers to keep off the chill during the cooler months.

2 Tapestry
A close cousin of embroidery, tapestry has been produced on the island ever since the 1890s. Kits are available for amateur enthusiasts.

3 Wicker
Centred around Camacha, Madeira's wickerworkers create at least 1,200 different articles.

4 Wine and Liqueurs
As well as fortified Madeira wine, the island produces *poncha,* a potent blend of sugarcane rum, honey and lemon juice.

5 Cork
Bags and shoes made of cork are a Portuguese speciality.

6 Pottery
Another speciality is pottery in Moorish designs, or shaped like cabbage leaves.

7 Cakes
Festive *bolo de mel* (honey cake), once made only at Christmas, is now a year-round treat, made using cane sugar, nuts and fruit.

8 Flowers
Colourful and long-lasting blooms are a good souvenir of this garden isle.

9 Artisanal chocolate
A box of chocolate truffles blended with Madeiran fruits will make for a delicious souvenir (see p24).

10 Embroidery
Now highly regarded by couturiers, Madeiran embroidery had unlikely beginnings; it was started by Bella Phelps in 1844 to provide work during a slump in the wine trade.

Traditional embroidered ornament

10 Madeira for Free

Viewing platform at Cabo Girão

1 Cabo Girão

At 580 m (1,903 ft), the highest sea cliff *(see p81)* in Madeira is impressive. The viewing platform at the top gives a dizzying panorama below – because the floor is made of glass – as well as out across the cliff edge. If you suffer from vertigo, don't even think about venturing on to it.

2 Mercado dos Lavradores

Arrive early and browse the fruit and vegetable stalls on the ground floor of this market *(see pp24–5)*. You may be offered a free slice of mango or custard apple to try. Afterwards, head for the basement and the busy fish market. Upstairs, look for the wines and liqueurs – free tastings are not uncommon.

3 Parque Florestal das Queimadas

MAP H3 ■ Sitio das Queimadas, Santana ■ Open daily

The thatched houses in this forest park look straight out of a fairytale. Set in Santana, Queimadas *(see p81)* is the ideal place to wander through the *laurissilva* forest and the perfect starting point for a hike to Pico das Pedras. Part of the trail is accessible for people in wheelchairs.

4 Funchal Cathedral (Sé)

The plain exterior of Funchal's cathedral *(see pp12–13)* belies an extraordinarily rich interior of paintings, statues and gilded chapels. The highlight is the knotwork ceiling, one of the richest and most elaborate in Portugal, which blends Moorish and European design elements.

5 Igreja do Colégio Guided Walking Tour

MAP P3 ■ Rua dos Ferreiros 11, Funchal ■ 291 705 060 ■ Open 10am–6pm Mon–Fri, 3–6pm Sat, 9am–1pm & 6:30–8:30pm Sun ■ www.madeiranheritage.pt

The ornate basalt façade of this 17th-century Jesuit church *(see p46)* is a treat. The interior has finely detailed frescoes, gilded filigree carvings and rare glazed tiles, design hallmarks of the Jesuit brotherhood. Visitors can choose between two tours – a free, 20-minute tour or a 1.5-hour long tour, which costs €5. Both can be booked online.

6 Traditional Santana Houses

MAP H2 ■ Rua do Sacristão, Santana ■ Open 10am–6pm daily

These wonderful A-frame houses *(see p82)*, with their square windows and scarlet doors, are compact and cosy. The island's tourist-board examples in Santana have been well preserved within trim gardens, their thatched roofs and painted doorways still in pristine condition.

Traditional Santana house

7 Fortaleza de São Filipe Ruins

MAP P4 ■ Praça da Autonomia, Funchal

The ruins of this fortress wall, built in 1581, are set between the Santa Luzia and João Gomes streams. Nearby, the foundations of outhouses and the remains of a mid-16th-century cistern can also be admired.

8 Fortaleza de São Tiago

The São Tiago fortress marks the boundary of the Zona Velha. Built to repel pirate attack, the stronghold is a good place for kids to run about. The views out across the Atlantic are stupendous, and there are a couple of good places to eat in and around the building. Ideal for a day trip.

9 Capela do Corpo Santo

This simple chapel in the Zona Velha *(see pp22–3)* was built in the 15th century, though what you see today is largely 16th century. It was made by a charity that raised funds for local fishermen and their families, who didn't have enough money to buy food or take shelter.

10 Palácio de São Lourenço Guided Walking Tour

Dating from 1513, this beautiful fortress-palace was the residence of Madeira's military island governors up to 1834. Its rooms brim with Portuguese and European decorative art, and there is also an exhibition about the fort's history *(see p76)*. The walking tour is suitable for all levels of fitness.

🔟 Festivals

1 Carnival
Funchal ■ Feb–Mar (47 days before Easter)

Celebrated over three days before Shrove Tuesday, Carnival is when schools, clubs and bands parade down the streets in fancy dress, followed by a colourful allegorical parade on the last day. Not as wild as Rio, but still an excuse to let your hair down.

Glamorous carnival costumes

2 Flower Festival
Funchal ■ Apr/May

The floats come out again for the spring Flower Festival in April or May. This was originally created as a tourist attraction, but now it is a festival that Madeirans have taken to their heart, with passionate competition among local clubs to produce the best float.

Pretty float at the Flower Festival

3 Atlantic Festival
Funchal ■ Jun

Held throughout June, the Festival do Atlântico combines fireworks, street entertainment and a music festival. There are performances by international stars as well as the accomplished local musicians from the Orquestra Clássica da Madeira, the Orquestra de Mandolins and the Funchal Brass Ensemble.

4 Jazz Festival
Funchal ■ First week of Jul

Staged in Santa Catarina Park (see p50), this prestigious three-day event, held in the first week of July, attracts some of the most famous names in international jazz, such as Jean Luc Ponty and Kenny Garret. Musicians include artists from Madeira and mainland Portugal. Jam sessions are staged at venues around Funchal to accompany the main programme.

5 Assumption in Monte
Monte, Funchal ■ 15 Aug

The Virgin is greatly revered by pious Madeirans because they believe she takes pity on human suffering. The day on which the Virgin is believed to have been assumed into heaven, 15 August, is observed in Monte (see pp34–5) with religious services and elaborate processions by day, and feasting, live music and a lot of dancing by night.

⑥ Columbus Festival
Vila Baleira ■ Early Sep

Costumed parades, street theatre, concerts and exhibitions in Porto Santo's tiny capital, Vila Baleira (see p101), re-create Columbus's arrival.

⑦ Feast of Bom Jesus
Ponta Delgada ■ First Sun of Sep

Pilgrims from all over the island come to Ponta Delgada (see p84) during this important religious festival to pray to the Bom Jesus ("Good Jesus"), a Christ figure believed to have miraculous powers.

⑧ Wine Festival
Estreito de Câmara de Lobos ■ Mid-Sep

The grape harvest is celebrated in Estreito de Câmara de Lobos with folk music and demonstrations of grape-crushing done with bare feet.

Crushing grapes at the Wine Festival

⑨ Nature Festival
Funchal ■ Second week of Oct

This festival promotes Madeira's natural resources and the best way to experience them on land, on sea or in the air. The initiative links sports and outdoor activities with ethnography and Madeiran culture.

⑩ Christmas and New Year
Regionwide ■ Dec

In December churches and shops mount cribs filled with traditional figures, such as rustic shepherds. The New Year's Eve fireworks have been recognized by Guinness Book of Records as the world's largest.

TOP 10 FESTIVE TRADITIONS

Typical *bolo do caco* bread

1 Bolo do Caco
Barbecued kebabs are eaten with spongy *bolo do caco* bread, a soft leavened flatbread, baked on the top of a stone oven.

2 Barbecues
No village festival is complete without delicious beef kebabs, barbecued in an old oil barrel.

3 Wine
Festivals are also a chance to sample local wines (and cider) that are not sold commercially.

4 Street Decorations
When streets are turned into tunnels of flowers, it's a sure sign that a festival is on the way.

5 Festive Greenery
Flower garlands are hung from poles wrapped in branches of sweet bay.

6 Flags and Light Bulbs
Bright white bulbs light up the night, and Madeira's flag – a red cross on a white background – is everywhere.

7 Firecrackers
Exploding firecrackers mark the start of a village festival (or a victory by one of the local football teams).

8 Processions and Sermons
Before the fun begins, the serious bit: a religious service to honour the patron saint.

9 Wall of Hope
At the Flower Festival, children make a wish and pin posies to a board in front of the town hall.

10 Music and Dance
Bands known as *filarmónicas*, which are formed of brass, accordian and wind instruments, provide the music for dancing the night away.

Madeira
Area by Area

Striking views over the cliffs from
Ponta de São Lourenço

TOP 10 Funchal

Founded in 1425, Funchal was granted city status in 1508. Many of its finest historical buildings are still intact, despite floods, piracy and earthquakes. Named Funchal ("Fennel") because of the wild fennel plants found growing in abundance by the first settlers, Madeira's capital sits on the island's southern coast in a natural amphitheatre, hemmed in by cliffs to the east and west, and steep green mountains to the north. Its streets are paved with black-and-white mosaics, and lined by blue-flowered jacaranda trees. Numerous public parks and private gardens make this a festive city filled with heady scents and colours, where architecture and nature are delightfully combined.

Leda and the Swan in the Town Hall courtyard

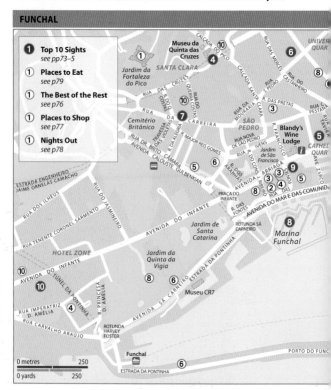

FUNCHAL

- ① Top 10 Sights
  see pp73–5
- ① Places to Eat
  see p79
- ① The Best of the Rest
  see p76
- ① Places to Shop
  see p77
- ① Nights Out
  see p78

1 Museu de Arte Sacra
MAP P3

The city's only open square is framed by the pretty Bishop's Palace, which houses the Museu de Arte Sacra (see pp14–15). Inaugurated in 1950, the museum features religious art, including a collection of 15th-century Flemish paintings. Across the square stands another landmark building, the graceful Baroque Câmara Municipal (see p44), Funchal's town hall.

Atmospheric streets, Zona Velha

2 Zona Velha
MAP P5

Funchal was the first Portuguese city to be founded outside the traditional boundaries of Europe, and the Zona Velha (see pp22–3) is where it all began. The original settlement was protected by the Fortaleza de São Tiago. Today, restaurants and bars line the rejuvenated Rua de Santa Maria and cluster around the Capela do Corpo Santo (see p23). A seafront promenade and park link the Zona Velha to the Monte cable car station (see p35) and the covered Mercado dos Lavradores (see pp24–5). The Zona Velha also houses the Madeira Story Centre (see p23).

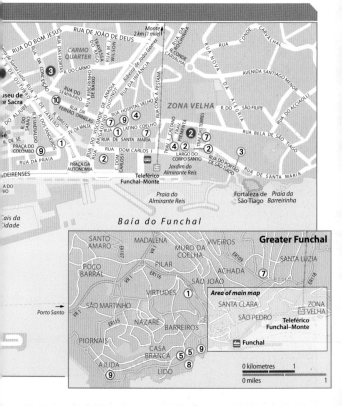

CALÇADA PAVEMENTS

The pavements of Funchal are works of art. Blocks of basalt and limestone are laid in intricate mosaic patterns, from the fish-scale design of the Town Hall square to the heraldic and floral motifs along Avenida Arriaga. The mosaics along Rua João Tavira depict the city's coat of arms – a wine carrier and the ship that brought Zarco (see p19).

 Carmo Quarter
MAP N4

The Carmo Quarter lies between two of the three creeks that flow through Funchal. Their deep channels across the city were once overhung with purple and red bougainvillea. Linking the 17th-century Carmo Church, the Franco Museum (see p48) and IVBAM is a warren of narrow streets, with fine buildings like the House of the Consuls (see p44).

 Santa Clara and São Pedro
MAP N2

It's worth climbing the steep Calçada de Santa Clara to reach the Museu da Quinta das Cruzes (see pp18–19). The museum houses a collection of decorative artwork and features well-manicured grounds that visitors can explore. Nearby are the serene Convento de Santa Clara (see pp20–21) and the Casa Museu Frederico de Freitas (see p48). Located north of Rua da Carreira in Rua Mouraria is the lovely church of São Pedro (see p46).

Interior of the church of São Pedro

 Cathedral Quarter
MAP P3

One of the few structures to have survived virtually intact since the early period of colonization in the 15th century, Funchal Cathedral (see pp12–13) was built with huge blocks of volcanic rocks that were transported from the cliffs at Cabo Girão (see p81). Today, the cathedral marks Funchal's social heart, the Cathedral Quarter, which is characterized by sociable bars and cafés, historic buildings including the Bank of Portugal (see p45) and the Alfândega (see p45).

 University Quarter
MAP N2

Statues of Jesuit saints stand in niches in the façade of the Igreja do Colégio (see p46), the huge and ornate church whose ancient school buildings are now the administrative offices of the University of Madeira (see p45). On the six city blocks to the north and on either side of these offices, you will find old-fashioned bookshops, cobbled wine lodges (see p62) and some of the city's oldest and most ornate tower houses.

 Rua da Carreira
MAP P2

Funchal was once known as "Little Lisbon", and the elegant buildings on Rua da Carreira, with their green shutters and iron balconies hung with plants, are a taste of the Portuguese capital. At the western end, a pretty casa de prazer (garden gazebo) sits on the corner of Rua do Quebra Costas, the street that leads to the secluded gardens of the Igreja Inglesa (see p44).

⑧ Seafront and Marina
MAP Q3

Everything in Funchal looks out to the sparkling sea and busy harbour, where private yachts, container ships and cruise liners on transatlantic voyages call in. Damaged by floods in 2010, the port and marina have now been completely redeveloped. Stroll along Avenida do Mar in the sunshine, and sample coffee and cakes at the kiosks along the seafront.

Yachts moored in Funchal's marina

⑨ Around Avenida Arriaga
MAP P2

Wide and leafy Avenida Arriaga is lined with some of Funchal's most prestigious public buildings, including Blandy's Wine Lodge (see pp16–17), one of the most popular visitor attractions on the island. Set within a 17th-century Franciscan friary, the lodge traces the history of Madeira wine and offers guided tours, in various languages, that uncork the secrets behind the production of one of the world's most famous wines. Situated nearby are Jardim de São Francisco (see p51) and the imposing Palácio de São Lourenço (see p76).

⑩ Hotel Zone
MAP Q1

West of the city, a succession of parks (see p50) and Art Deco mansions from the 1920s and 1930s line the Avenida do Infante. As the road crosses the ravine of the Ribeira Seco ("Dry River") and curves past Reid's Palace (see p115), mansions give way to big hotels along the clifftops, along with shopping centres and restaurants.

A DAY IN OLD FUNCHAL

▶ MORNING

Arrive for around 9am at **Mercado dos Lavradores** (see pp24–5), perhaps for a coffee and *bolo do caco* (see p61) at the rooftop Macaronésia café, before heading downstairs to the market.

Next, head for the **Madeira Story Centre** (see p23) for an overview of the island and its history and culture. While you're in this area you can explore the **Zona Velha** (see pp22–5) and wander the Jardim do Almirante Reis. Afterwards double back until you reach the **Funchal Cathedral** (see pp12–13). This will introduce you to the two main styles of Madeiran church architecture: both 16th-century Gothic and 18th-century Baroque.

For a break or a bite to eat, enjoy Funchal's laid-back café life in one of the eateries on Rua João Tavira and Rua da Sé.

AFTERNOON

Walk off your lunch by strolling along **Avenida Arriaga** until the Jardim Municipal. From here it's an uphill amble along Calçada de Santa Clara to the **Museu da Quinta das Cruzes** (see pp18–19). Allow at least an hour to explore the museum and its leafy archaeological gardens. On the way back down you'll pass the engaging **Casa Museu Frederico de Freitas** (see p48), which is worth half an hour.

Arrive back on Avenida Arriaga before 4:30pm for a guided tour of **Blandy's Wine Lodge** (see pp16–17), with wine tastings.

See map on pp72–3 ←

The Best of the Rest

1 Fortaleza do Pico
MAP N1 ■ Rua do Castelo ■ Open 10am–6pm Mon–Sat

It's an uphill slog from the centre to this undervisited fortress, but the views across the city are worth it. Still partly used by the military, but certain parts are open to the public.

2 Casa da Luz – Museu de Electricidade
This former power station (see p22) explores the heroic efforts that were needed to bring electricity to the island. Some of the huge machinery required is on display.

3 Madeira Optics Museum
MAP P2 ■ Rua das Pretas 51 ■ 291 220 694/961 822 358 ■ Open 10am–1pm & 3–7pm Mon–Fri, 10am–1pm Sat ■ Adm ■ www.madeiraopticsmuseum.com

More than 2,000 optic-related items are on display here, including telescopes, binoculars and cameras.

4 Art of Open Doors
This project (see p22) has meant that the doors in Madeira's oldest street have been decorated with striking designs. The work was carried out by a range of local and international artists in a variety of styles.

5 Palácio de São Lourenço
MAP P3 ■ Avenida Zarco ■ 291 204 902 ■ Open 10am–4:30pm Mon–Fri ■ Adm

This historic fortress houses the engaging Museu Militar da Madeira.

6 History Tellers
MAP H5 ■ Rua dos Ferreiros ■ 935 010 779 ■ www.madeiran heritage.pt

Informative walking tours recounting Madeira's colourful past, led by students from the University of Madeira.

7 Artesanato da Madeira
MAP N3 ■ Rua dos Ferreiros 152 ■ 291 204 600 ■ Open 10am–12:30pm, 2–5:30pm Mon–Fri

Traditional handicrafts as well as contemporary artifacts are on sale at this authentic venue. A themed exhibition complements the merchandise.

8 Madeira Film Experience
MAP Q2 ■ Marina Shopping, Rua Conselheiro José Silvestre 1 ■ 291 222 748 ■ Open 10:15am–5:30pm daily ■ www.madeirafilmexperience.com

This packs 600 years of history and culture into an entertaining, 30-minute audiovisual experience

9 Museu do Brinquedo
From 19th-century china dolls to 1980s Barbies, this museum (see p22) has over 100 years of toy history, with a huge collection of miniature cars. There is a restaurant on site too.

10 Universo de Memórias João Carlos Abreu
MAP N2 ■ Santa Clara Civic and Cultural Centre, Calçada do Pico 2 ■ 291 225 122 ■ Open 10am–5pm Mon–Fri ■ Adm

A thought-provoking exhibition of memorabilia collected by traveller, writer, politician and artist João Carlos Abreu.

Palácio de São Lourenço

Places to Shop

1 Fábrica do Ribeiro Sêco
MAP G5 ▪ Rua das Maravilhas
170 ▪ Open 9am–1pm & 2–6pm Mon–
Fri ▪ www.fabricaribeiroseco.com
This mill produces and sells classic
and organic cane honey as well as
honey cakes and biscuits. Visitors
can also tour the facility, which is
situated on the sugar cane and
rum route of Madeira.

2 Casa do Turista
All the elegance of a bygone
era can be found at Casa do Turista
(see p65): Madeiran and mainland
Portuguese textiles, ceramics, silver
and glassware, tableware and
handmade cloth dolls.

3 Galerias São Lourenço
MAP P2 ▪ Avenida Arriaga 41
Funchal's most upmarket shopping
mall, offering everything from
sunglasses and children's clothes
to elegant kitchen- and tableware.

4 Armazém do Mercado
This is a series of pop-up
local business enterprises *(see p23)*.
Visitors can shop for organic produce
as well as quirky souvenirs. There
are a number of quality eateries
located here, too.

5 La Vie Shopping Centre
MAP P1 ▪ Rua Dr Brito Câmara 9
La Vie boasts a city centre location
and eye-catching architecture. It
houses fashion boutiques, jewellers,
leisurewear and sports shops, as
well as a hypermarket.

**6 Design Center Nini
Andrade Silva**
MAP H6 ▪ Estrada da Pontinha, Forte
de Nossa Senhora da Conceição ▪ 291
648 780 ▪ Open 11am–7pm daily
▪ www.niniandradesilva.com
Funchal-born interior designer Nini
Andrade Silva has created several
Madeira hotel interiors. Here her
work is showcased alongside a
smart restaurant.

Mercado dos Lavradores

7 Mercado dos Lavradores
Make it a habit while in Funchal
to visit the market *(see pp24–5)* and
shop for picnic ingredients or souvenirs, or to savour the colourful bustle.

8 Livraria Esperança
MAP N3 ▪ Rua dos Ferreiros
119 ▪ 291 221 116 ▪ Open 9am–7pm
Mon–Fri
A cavernous homage to all things
literary, this claims to be Portugal's
largest bookshop with over 100,000
new and secondhand titles. Seek out
the good foreign-language section.

9 Forum Madeira
MAP G6 ▪ Estrada Monumental
390, Lido
A stylish mall, Forum Madeira
houses over 80 stores, a giant
hypermarket, 17 restaurants and
six cinemas. Sea views can be
enjoyed from the rooftop terrace.

10 Rua Dr. Fernão Ornelas
MAP P4
This attractive pedestrianized street
is a wonderful mix of chic boutiques
sitting cheek-by-jowl with grocers
selling coffee and pungent salt cod.
Most shops close on Saturday
afternoon and Sunday.

See map on pp72–3 ←

Nights Out

Exterior of 23 Vintage Bar

1 23 Vintage Bar

MAP Q6 ■ Rua de Santa Maria 27 ■ 914 758 975 ■ Open 5pm–1am Tue–Thu, 8pm–4am Sat & Sun

This late-night bar is a popular spot, with music of the 1970s, 80s and 90s.

2 Venda Velha

MAP Q6 ■ Rua de Santa Maria 170 ■ 925 003 460 ■ Open noon–4am daily; winter hours may vary

Madeira's potent tipple, *poncha (see p65)*, is served with gusto at this bar. On Friday and Saturday nights, the revelry spills out on to the terrace.

3 Teatro Municipal

MAP P2 ■ Avenida Arriaga ■ 291 215 130

This resplendent theatre (built 1888) hosts music recitals, contemporary dance, drama (usually in Portuguese) as well as art-house movies. Look for billboards outside the theatre telling you what's on.

4 Café do Teatro

MAP P2 ■ Avenida Arriaga 40 ■ 924 437 951

The romantic night-time haunt of Funchal's smart set, this small but sophisticated café offers cocktails, chat and occasional DJs.

5 Hole in One

MAP G6 ■ Estrada Monumental 238 A ■ 291 765 443 ■ www.holein onemadeira.com

Enjoy live music sessions with a pint of Guinness or the local Coral beer at this Irish pub.

6 Discoteca Vespas

MAP Q2 ■ Avenida Sá Carneiro 7 (opposite the container port) ■ 291 234 800

At Madeira's best-known disco, three clubs under the same roof cater to a youthful crowd of locals and tourists.

7 Sabor a Fado

MAP P5 ■ Travessa das Torres 10 ■ 925 612 259

Pleasant restaurant with live music by the waiting staff and an authentic and traditional Portuguese menu.

8 Casino da Madeira

MAP H6 ■ Avenida do Infante ■ 291 140 424 ■ Open 3pm–3am Sun–Thu, 4pm–4am Fri, Sat & bank holidays ■ www. casinodamadeira.com

Play slot machines, roulette and blackjack at this casino, or enjoy spectacular dinner shows and live music in the Copacabana Bar.

Casino da Madeira

9 Living Room

MAP P3 ■ Travessa dos Varadouros 4-8 ■ 925 633 919 ■ Open 10pm–2am Wed & Thu (to 4am Fri & Sat)

Funky boutique bar and dance club that's also an art gallery. Local DJs work in this micro space that's also a decent gin palace.

10 Classical Concerts

291 752 173 ■ www. madeiramandolin.com

Madeira's Mandolin Orchestra, the oldest mandolin orchestra in Europe, was founded in 1913. Check online for their upcoming performances.

See map on pp72–3

Places to Eat

1 Armazém do Sal
MAP P3 ▪ Rua da Alfândega 135 ▪ 919 134 411 ▪ Closed Sat lunch & Sun ▪ €€

Once used for storing salt, this former warehouse has been carefully transformed into a highly regarded upscale eatery. The smoked sea bass is excellent.

2 Gavião Novo
MAP Q6 ▪ Rua de Santa Maria 131, Funchal ▪ 291 229 238 ▪ €€

Famous for its fish and seafood, this restaurant (see p60) also offers creative meat dishes such as the fillet steak with Roquefort cheese.

3 Restaurante Lá ao Fundo
MAP P5 ▪ Rua Portão de São Tiago 17A ▪ 964 527 912 ▪ €€

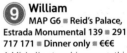

Il Gallo d'Oro

Set close to the fortress of São Tiago (see p22), this restaurant serves up a creative fusion of Mozambican and Goan dishes.

4 Dona Amélia
MAP Q1 ▪ Rua Imperatriz Dona Amélia 83 ▪ 291 225 784 ▪ Dinner only ▪ €€

A fine-dining restaurant (see p60) serving classic Mediterranean and regional dishes. Booking is advisable.

5 Avista
MAP G6 ▪ Estrada Monumental 145 ▪ 291 707 770 ▪ €€

Creative Mediterranean cuisine, an inspired wine list and stunning sea views combine to offer a romantic dining experience. An Asian menu is available Wednesday to Sunday.

6 UVA
MAP P2 ▪ Vine Hotel, Rua dos Aranhas 27 ▪ 291 009 000 ▪ Dinner only ▪ €€

Top-notch gastronomy with top-floor views, this hotel restaurant is also a wine bar. Excellent service.

PRICE CATEGORIES

For a three course meal for one with half a bottle of wine (or equivalent meal), taxes and extra charges.

€ under €25   €€ €25–€60   €€€ over €60

7 Tasca Literária Dona Joana Rabo-de-Peixe
MAP P5 ▪ Rua de Santa Maria 77 ▪ 291 220 348 ▪ €€

Try the Guacamole à "Remelico" at this quirky tapas bar (see p61).

8 Il Gallo d'Oro
MAP G6 ▪ Cliff Bay Hotel, Estrada Monumental 147 ▪ 291 707 700 ▪ Closed Sun ▪ €€€

This sophisticated dining venue (see p60) has two Michelin stars.

9 William
MAP G6 ▪ Reid's Palace, Estrada Monumental 139 ▪ 291 717 171 ▪ Dinner only ▪ €€€

A Michelin star shines over this gourmet restaurant (see p60) with fabulous ocean views.

10 Beef and Wines
MAP H6 ▪ Edifício Infante Dom Henrique 60, Avenida do Infante ▪ 291 282 257 ▪ Open 7–11pm Mon–Sat (noon–3pm & 7–11pm Thu) ▪ €€€

This restaurant serves Brazilian dishes such as picanha (grilled rump of beef) and feijoada (black-bean stew), some fish and seafood.

Interior of Beef and Wines

TOP10 Central Madeira

Traditional home, Santana

The centre of Madeira consists mainly of high volcanic peaks and deep ravines. To experience this scenery to the full, it is best to walk, but thanks to well-placed *miradouros* (scenic viewing points), you can take some memorable photographs and enjoy the visual appeal of the central mountain range even when travelling by road. There are great contrasts between the north and south. Soaked in sunshine, the southern slopes are densely populated, with red-tiled farmhouses in a sea of vines and bananas. The northern slopes are densely wooded; along the coastal strip, tiny terraces cling to the steep valley sides.

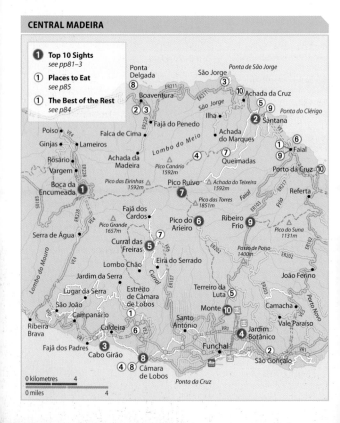

CENTRAL MADEIRA

- **1** Top 10 Sights
  see pp81–3
- **1** Places to Eat
  see p85
- **1** The Best of the Rest
  see p84

0 kilometres 4

0 miles 4

1 Boca da Encumeada

The Encumeada Pass is a saddle of rock dividing the north and south of the island. Clouds from the north often spill over the tips of the mountains. There are majestic peaks, from Pico Grande in the east to cone-shaped Crista do Galo in the west. Just south of the pass is the Levada do Norte *(see p54)*.

2 Santana

MAP H2 ■ Horários do Funchal bus 56, Carros de São Gonçalo bus 103
Santana has Madeira's best examples of the traditional timber-and-thatch dwellings known as *palheiros*. These brightly-painted triangular houses are comfortable but compact, and many now have modern extensions to accommodate the kitchens and bathrooms that the originals lacked. You can visit a row of tourist-board houses next to the church, but in the lanes of the village you will see plenty more, with very tidy gardens.

3 Cabo Girão

MAP E5 ■ Rodoeste buses 6, 7 & 142
Madeira's highest sea cliff, 580 m (1,903 ft) above the ocean, also claims to be the second highest in the world. From the glass-floored viewing point, you gaze down on to a *fajã*, a rock platform created when the cliff face fell into the sea millennia ago. Local farmers cultivate crops here in neat terraces. For a closer look, take the cable car *(teleférico)* from Caldeira Rancho, on the western side of Câmara de Lobos, to the base of the cliff.

4 Jardim Botânico

Visit Jardim Botânico *(see pp26–7)* to satisfy your curiosity about the names and origins of all the flowering trees, palms, succulents and scented climbers that grow everywhere in Madeira – in front gardens of houses, in public parks and along country roads.

Topiary at Jardim Botânico

5 Curral das Freiras

A long road-tunnel now links the valley village of Curral das Freiras *(see pp36–7)* with the wider world, the old road having been closed due to safety concerns. Upon arrival in "Nun's Refuge", you gain a sense of just how isolated this community once was.

Curral das Freiras

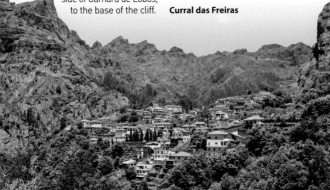

6 Pico do Arieiro

In the colourful landscape of Madeira's third highest peak *(see pp38–9)*, you can read the story of the volcanic forces that created the island, and the elemental battles between wind, rock and rain that eroded it into the jagged peaks and plunging ravines that visitors see today.

Hiking path, Pico do Arieiro

7 Pico Ruivo

MAP G3 ■ No bus

Madeira's highest peak is reached from the road next to the petrol station on the eastern side of Santana. This leads to the car park at Achada do Teixeira, from where a well-paved path climbs to the summit (1,862 m/ 6,109 ft). To the south, the views look over the high peaks and jagged

---

A-FRAME HOUSES

The colourful A-frame houses *(see p66)* of the Santana district were probably introduced by early settlers from the farming districts of central Portugal. Today, they are used as houses, or as cattle byres. On an island of precipitous slopes, cattle can easily fall if left to graze freely, so they are kept in the cool shade of the thatched *palheiros*, to which their owners carry stacks of freshly cut grass and foliage at regular intervals during the day.

---

ridges of an arid volcanic landscape; to the north, clouds hang around the lush, forested slopes. Back at the car park, look out for the eroded rocks called Homem em Pé ("Standing Man") that can be seen in a hollow behind the rest house.

8 Câmara de Lobos

MAP F6 ■ All Rodoeste buses

The *lobos* ("wolves") in the name of this pretty village refer to the monk seals that once basked on the pebbly beach. This area is now used as an open-air boatyard, where traditional craft are repaired or given a fresh coat of blue, red and yellow paint, laid on in bold stripes. Down among the noisy bars is the Fishermen's Chapel, where villagers give thanks for the safe return of their men after a long night at sea, fishing for *espada* (scabbard fish), most of which is served up on the tables of Madeira's many restaurants. Admire the bay from Pico da Torre or continue to Estreito de Câmara de Lobos.

Harbour and colourful boats at Câmara de Lobos

9 Ribeiro Frio
MAP H4 ■ São Roque do Faial ■ Horários do Funchal bus 56, Carros de São Gonçalo bus 103

This valley clearing's "Cold River" tumbles down the mountain to bring clear water to a trout farm in a pretty garden. Some of the trout end up on the menu of the Restaurante Ribeiro Frio opposite, a good place to begin or end a short walk along the dry *levada* to Balcões. The longer Levada do Furado walk to Portela starts here too; you need a map to do the whole route, but you can enjoy views of the UNESCO-listed *laurissilva* forest in the surrounding Ribeiro Frio Forest Park by doing just the first stretch.

Clear waters of the Ribeiro Frio

10 Monte
Take the cable car up from Funchal's Zona Velha to Monte *(see pp34–5)*, and you will sail 600 m (1,968 ft) up the southern face of Madeira to a place that seems more garden than village, shaded by tall trees and watered by natural springs.

A DAY IN CENTRAL MADEIRA

▶ MORNING

Starting in **Monte** by 10am at the latest, head first to the summit of **Pico do Arieiro** (if it's too cloudy, do the trip in reverse; the weather may clear later on).

Afterwards, descend to **Ribeiro Frio** to visit the trout farm and enjoy the native Madeiran flowers in the surrounding gardens.

Walk downhill past the shop, and take the *levada* path signposted left to **Balcões** *(see p55)*. A 20-minute stroll through woodland brings you to a cutting in the rock that affords wonderful views over the island's central peaks and valleys.

For lunch, try the small café at Ribeiro Frio. If you prefer to bring your own food, there are picnic areas in the vicinity. Alternatively, continue on to **Santana** *(see p81)*.

AFTERNOON

If you're not already in Santana, make your way there to see the traditional triangular houses and the **Madeira Theme Park** *(see p58)*. Next, follow signs to the Rocha do Navio Teleférico, and you will find a cable car and footpath to **Santana's beach**.

Now head west into **Faial** *(see p84)*. Two "balconies" along the way give you memorable views of **Penha de Águia** *(see p84)*.

If you're staying in Funchal, the fastest route back is to follow signs to Machico through a long tunnel that links up with the airport road back to the city.

See map on p80

The Best of the Rest

1 **São Roque do Faial**
MAP J3

Several valleys meet at São Roque, so walkers can start at the church and choose one of the paths that go west up the Ribeiro Frio ("Cold River") or east up the Tem-te Não Caias (literally, "Hold On; Don't Fall").

2 **Boaventura**
MAP G2

If you want to explore the orchards watered by the Levada de Cima, Boaventura makes a great base. Take a good walking guide with you.

3 **São Jorge**
MAP H2

A Baroque church from 1761 stands in São Jorge, and Ponta de São Jorge has a 19th-century lighthouse with coast views. A side road east of the village leads to a small, sheltered beach *(see p53)*.

Lighthouse on Ponta de São Jorge

4 **Caldeirão Verde**
MAP G3

From Queimadas, a scenic *levada* walk leads to the "Green Cauldron", a waterfall cascading down a rock hollow. Sturdy footwear, torches (flashlights) and waterproofs are needed.

5 **Terreiro da Luta**
MAP H5

Pious Madeirans believe that the Virgin appeared to a young shepherd girl on this spot and gave her the statue now in Monte church. The memorial, on Caminho dos Pretos, was erected after 1916.

Eagle Rock or Penha de Águia

6 **Penha de Águia**
MAP J3

"Eagle Rock" rises 590 m (1,935 ft) from the sea, casting its shadow over neighbouring villages. Young Madeirans regard the climb from Penha de Águia de Baixo to the top as a test of strength and endurance.

7 **Queimadas**
MAP H3

From western Santana, a road signposted to "Queimadas" gives way to a track leading to a house with gardens, ponds and picnic tables in the heart of the UNESCO World Natural Heritage forest.

8 **Ponta Delgada**
MAP F2

Popular for its seafront saltwater swimming pools *(see p53)* and regional handicrafts *(see p65)*, this small village also boasts a beautiful church that is worth a visit.

9 **Faial**
MAP J3

The Fortim do Faial is a toy-town fort built in the 18th century to fend off pirates. South of the village are views of Penha de Águia and an area where part of the cliff fell into the sea.

10 **Porto da Cruz**
MAP J3

The Old Town is a maze of cobbled alleys. A sugar mill stands by the harbour, where visitors can buy the locally distilled spirit *aguardente*.

See map on p80

Places to Eat

1 **Adega da Quinta, Estreito de Câmara de Lobos**

MAP F5 ▪ Quinta do Estreito, Rua José Joaquim da Costa ▪ 291 910 530 ▪ €€

Rustic Madeiran food is the speciality at this hotel restaurant. Sample the succulent *espetada* (meat kebab), roasted in a wood-burning oven.

2 **Casa Velha**

MAP H6 ▪ Casa Velha do Palheiro, Rua da Estalagem 23, São Gonçalo ▪ 291 790 350 ▪ €€

A stately charm pervades this country style dining room, all Villeroy & Boch tableware and floral trim. Expect haute cuisine and fine wines.

3 **São Cristóvão, Boaventura**

MAP F2 ▪ Sitio de São Cristóvão ▪ 291 862 066 ▪ Closed Mon ▪ €€

Along the northern central coast, this traditional Portuguese eatery has a good view of the sea and mountains.

4 **Vila do Peixe**

MAP F6 ▪ Rua Dr João Abel de Freitas, Câmara de Lobos ▪ 291 099 909 ▪ €€

The menu at this restaurant *(see p60)* features the day's catch, simply prepared and served with a lovely harbour view.

5 **Churrascaria Caldeirão Verde, Santana**

MAP H2 ▪ Avenida Manuel Marques da Trindade ▪ 291 576 185 ▪ €

A great stand-by with no-frills service but excellent value grilled steak and skewered meats *(espetada)*.

6 **Churrascaria O Lagar, Câmara de Lobos**

MAP F6 ▪ Estrada do João G Zarco 478 ▪ 291 941 865 ▪ €€

A big palace in the hills serving tender garlic-flavoured chicken and skewers of beef, with warm *bolo do caco* bread.

PRICE CATEGORIES

For a three course meal for one with half a bottle of wine (or equivalent meal), taxes and extra charges.

€ under €25 ▪ €€ €25–€60 ▪ €€€ over €60

7 **Sabores do Curral, Curral das Freiras**

MAP F4 ▪ Caminho da Igreja 1 ▪ 291 712 257 ▪ Closed Mon ▪ €€

This charming, rustic eatery offers traditional gastronomical delights of local produce with chestnut as the main ingredient. Try the liqueur.

8 **Vila da Carne**

MAP F6 ▪ Rua Dr. João Abel de Freitas, Câmara de Lobos ▪ 291 099 908 ▪ €€

Housed in the same space as Vila do Peixe, the restaurant is all about various meats. Sizzling *espetada* is the signature dish.

9 **Cantinho da Serra**

MAP H2 ▪ Estrada do Pico das Pedras 57, Santana ▪ 291 573 727 ▪ €€

Hearty home cooking reinforces the warm, rustic ambience at Cantinho da Serra *(see p61)*. In winter they heat the room with an inviting log fire.

10 **Quinta do Furão**

MAP H2 ▪ Estrada Quinta do Furão 6 ▪ 291 570 100 ▪ €€

A combination of traditional Madeiran flavours and international influences is carefully prepared at this restaurant *(see p61)*. Great terrace views.

The terrace at Quinta do Furão

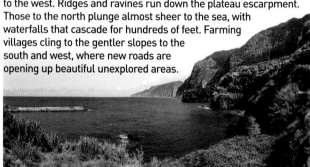 Western Madeira

The Valley Road linking Ribeira Brava and São Vicente via the Encumeada Pass forms the boundary between the high peaks of central Madeira and the flat moorland of the Paúl da Serra plateau to the west. Ridges and ravines run down the plateau escarpment. Those to the north plunge almost sheer to the sea, with waterfalls that cascade for hundreds of feet. Farming villages cling to the gentler slopes to the south and west, where new roads are opening up beautiful unexplored areas.

Panoramic view of the dramatic cliffs at the bay of Seixal

WESTERN MADEIRA

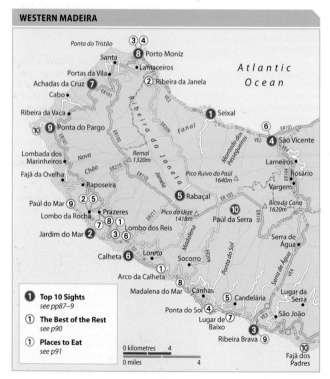

Ponta do Tristão
Santa
Portas da Vila
Achadas da Cruz ⑦
Cabo
Ribeira da Vaca
⑩ ⑨ Ponta do Pargo
Lombada dos Marinheiros
Nova
Fajã da Ovelha
Chão
Raposeira
Paúl do Mar ② ⑤
Lombo da Rocha
Prazeres
Jardim do Mar ②
⑦ ⑧ ① Lombo dos Reis
③ ⑥
Calheta ⑥
Loreto
Arco da Calheta ①
Madalena do Mar
Ponta do Sol ④

③ ④
⑧ Porto Moniz
Lamaceiros
② Ribeira da Janela
Remal 1320m
Pico Ruivo do Paúl 1640m
⑤ Rabaçal
Pico do Urze 1418m
Socorro
Canhas
⑤ Candelária
Lugar de Baixo
Ribeira Brava ⑨

① Seixal
⑥ ER101
④ São Vicente
Lameiros
Rosário
Vargem
Bica da Cana 1620m
⑩ Paúl da Serra
Serra de Água
Lugar da Serra
São João
Fajã dos Padres ⑩

Atlantic Ocean

Ribeira da Janela / Fanal / Jonela / Madalena / Ponta do Sol / Serra de Água (map labels)
Montado dos Pessegueiros

① Top 10 Sights
see pp87–9

① The Best of the Rest
see p90

① Places to Eat
see p91

0 kilometres 4
0 miles 4

1 Seixal
MAP D2 ■ Rodoeste bus 139

Most of the coastal road now runs through tunnels, but from Seixal you can get a sense of the north coast's visual splendour. Tall cliffs stretching into the distance are pounded by powerful waves. Vineyards cling to the rock on almost vertical terraces. Waterfalls plunge from the wooded heights on either side of the village.

2 Jardim do Mar
MAP B4 ■ Rodoeste buses 80 and 163

This pretty village (literally, "Garden of the Sea") sits at the meeting-point of ancient cobbled footpaths, which climb up the cliffs. In the village, a maze of alleys winds down to a pebble beach, where surfing competitions are held during the winter. A large sea-wall makes surfing here tricky, even for the very experienced.

3 Ribeira Brava
MAP D5 ■ Rodoeste buses 4, 6, 7, 80, 127, 139 and 142 ■ Museu Etnográfico da Madeira: Rua São Francisco 24; 291 952 598; open 9:30am–5pm Tue–Fri, 10am–12:30pm & 1:30–5:30pm Sat–Sun; adm

Ribeira Brava (literally, "Wild Stream") is one of the island's oldest towns, well established as a centre of sugar production by the 1440s. The parish church has a sculpture from the 1480s. The Museu Etnográfico da Madeira is worth a visit; it also has a crafts shop.

Large parish church of Ribeira Brava

Historical centre of São Vicente

4 São Vicente
MAP E2 ■ Rodoeste buses 6 and 139

This pretty village on the northern side of the Encumeada Pass would be wonderful to paint: deep-green shutters, doors and balconies, with stone lintels and frames of ox-blood red, are set in white-walled houses along the grey basalt streets.

5 Rabaçal
MAP C3

Washed by centuries of rain running from the flat surface of the Paúl da Serra, Rabaçal is a green cleft in the moorland. A brisk 2-km (1-mile) walk down a winding tarmac path goes through heather to a forest house with picnic tables. Rabaçal marks the start of two popular signposted walks. One follows the Levada do Risco to the Risco Waterfall (30 minutes there and back); the other leads down to 25 Fontes ("25 Springs"), a cauldron-like pool fed by many falls (1 hour 40 minutes there and back).

6 Calheta

MAP B4 ■ Rodoeste buses 80, 142, 163 and 164 ■ Calheta Church: open 10am–1pm & 4–6pm daily ■ Engenho da Calheta: 291 822 264; open 8am–7pm Tue–Sun

Standing on a terrace halfway up the hill leading west out of the village, Calheta's fine parish church is a scaled-down version of Funchal cathedral (see pp12–13). The church contains a precious 17th-century ebony-and-silver tabernacle, and a richly decorated *alfarge* (knotwork) ceiling above the high altar. Next door to the church is the Engenho da Calheta, one of Madeira's two surviving sugar mills; the other is in Porto da Cruz (see p84). As well as producing *mel* (honey), which is used in making the island's unique *bolo de mel* (honey cake), the mill also manufactures *aguardente* (rum) using distilled cane syrup.

Fields of Achadas da Cruz

7 Achadas da Cruz

MAP B2 ■ Cable car: Caminho do Teleférico, Achadas da Cruz ■ 291 852 951 ■ Open 8am–noon & 1–6pm daily ■ Adm

Little visited, perhaps due to a lack of signage, this corner of the island is worth making the effort to explore. The village is nondescript except for the fact that it is the departure point for one of the most memorable and knee-trembling cable car rides in Madeira. The gondola glides over the edge of a 450-m (1,476-ft) cliff to take you down to a rocky beach and a few huts below via a jaw-dropping view.

Rough seas and rocks at Porto Moniz

8 Porto Moniz

MAP C1 ■ Rodoeste buses 80 and 139

At the most northwesterly point on the island is Porto Moniz, which comprises a bustling agricultural town set high up around its church, with a lower town devoted to food and bathing. Natural rock pools have been turned into a bathing complex offering a safe environment in which to enjoy the exhilarating experience of being showered by spray from waves breaking on the offshore rocks. The landscaped seafront is lined with restaurants selling some of the island's best seafood.

9 Ponta do Pargo

MAP A2 ■ Rodoeste buses 80 and 142

Madeira's westernmost point, Ponta do Pargo is the best place on the island to watch the setting sun or to gaze down at the waves breaking along the cliffs of the island's coasts. The lighthouse set on the headland dates from the early 20th century and has a small exhibition of maps and photographs charting the history of lighthouses on every island in the Madeiran archipelago. The ceiling of the parish church depicts colourful sunsets, terraced hills, and the scenic spots of the western part of the island. They were all painted in the 1990s by a Belgian artist who settled in the village.

⑩ Paúl da Serra
MAP D3

The undulating plateau of Paúl da Serra ("Mountain Marsh") is where the waters that feed many of the island's streams and *levadas* gather. It acts as a sponge for the abundant rains that fall when clouds reach the island, rise, then cool. Free-range horned cattle graze the lush grass. People from the nearby villages pick wild bilberries and blackberries in summer, which they turn into tasty conserves. Many also depend on the plateau's wind turbines for electricity.

SUGAR REVIVAL

The sugar mills at Calheta and Porto da Cruz date from the sugar renaissance of the 19th century, when the demand for high-quality sugar increased dramatically, thanks to the popularity of sweetmeats in genteel European households. The nuns of Santa Clara (see p20) were especially renowned for their preserves, marzipan sweets, crystallized figs and other delights.

A DAY IN WESTERN MADEIRA

▶ MORNING

The first stop on this long but rewarding trip is **Ribeira Brava** (see p87), located 25 minutes from Funchal by the winding south coast highway. If you arrive before the Museu Etnográfico da Madeira opens, enjoy a coffee on the seafront or take a look inside the **São Bento** church (see p47). Driving north on the ER104 (VE4), follow signs to Serra de Água. For spectacular mountain views, avoid the highway tunnel route to **São Vicente** (see p87). Turn off along the way for refreshments at **Hotel Encumeada** (see p117) and absorb those jaw-dropping vistas. Descending to São Vicente, spare some time for a short but fascinating tour of the **Grutas de São Vicente** (see p58). For a good lunch head to the seafront and **O Cachalote** (see p91).

AFTERNOON

Porto Moniz can be reached via the modern highway, with the old ER101 (Antiga) coastal road deemed too dangerous due to rock falls. If it's hot, take a dip in the natural rock pools (see p53). Otherwise, take the ER110 for a pleasant undulating drive across the **Paúl da Serra** plateau. Pause at **Rabaçal** (see p87) and stretch your legs along the *levada* path that leads to a waterfall (see p55). Allow at least an hour to explore this woodland world. Head back via the Encumeada Pass to rejoin the ER104 (VE4) back to Funchal.

See map on p86 ←

The Best of the Rest

1 Arco da Calheta
MAP C4

An early church survives at the heart of this sprawling village. The Capela do Loreto, founded by the wife of Zarco's grandson, dates from the mid-15th century.

2 Ribeira da Janela
MAP C1

This wild, uninhabited valley joins the sea beside a rocky islet with a hole like a window (its name is "Window Valley"). The road descends through a misty world of ancient trees kept moist by the condensation of clouds.

Ribeira da Janela road

3 MUDAS Museu de Arte Contemporânea da Madeira
MAP B4 ■ Estrada Simão Gonçalves da Câmara 37 ■ 291 820 900 ■ Open 10am–5pm Tue–Sun ■ Adm

This minimalist cultural centre houses permanent as well as temporary exhibitions, an auditorium, a restaurant and a bookstore.

4 Ponta do Sol
MAP D5 ■ Rua Príncipe Dom Luís 3 ■ 291 974 034

The American novelist John dos Passos (1896–1970) visited this village in 1960 to see the home of his grandparents. The house has since been turned into a cultural centre.

5 Lombada
MAP D5

On a ridge above Ponta do Sol is one of Madeira's oldest houses – the 15th-century mansion of Columbus's friend João Esmeraldo. The watermill opposite is fed by one of the island's oldest *levadas*. A pretty church of 1722 is lined with tile pictures of the Virtues.

6 Lombo dos Reis
MAP B4

The "Ridge of the Kings" is named after the tiny, rustic Capela dos Reis Magos ("Chapel of the Three Kings"), with a 16th-century Flemish altar carving of the Nativity.

7 Lugar de Baixo
MAP D5

Above the tiny freshwater lagoon at Lugar de Baixo is a visitor centre with pictures of the wild birds that frequent this shore, though you will mostly see domesticated ducks and moorhens.

8 Prazeres
MAP B3

The priest at Prazeres has set up a small children's farm opposite the church. The main attraction is the flower-lined path along the Levada Nova (New Levada).

9 Paúl do Mar
MAP A3

The best approach to this fishing (and surfing) village is down the twisting road from Fajã de Ovelha. On the way, look out for a glimpse of the stunning Galinhas Gorge.

10 Fajã dos Padres
MAP E5 ■ Rua Padre António Dinis Henriques 1, Fajã dos Padres ■ 291 944 538 ■ www.fajados padres.com

A cable car carries visitors down to a restaurant on a pebble beach fronting vineyards and vegetable gardens.

→ *See map on p86*

Places to Eat

PRICE CATEGORIES

For a three course meal for one with half a bottle of wine (or equivalent meal), taxes and extra charges.

€ under €25 €€ €25–€60 €€€ over €60

1 Convento das Vinhas, Calheta

MAP B4 ▪ Caminho Lombo do Salão 35 ▪ 291 822 164 ▪ €€

This rustic family-run eatery offers classic Madeiran and Portuguese favourites, along with a local delicacy, *ovas de espada* (scabbard fish eggs).

2 Jardim Atlântico, Prazeres

MAP B3 ▪ Lombo da Rocha ▪ 291 820 220 ▪ €€

The best bet for vegetarians looking for an escape from an endless diet of omelettes, the restaurant at the Jardim Atlântico Hotel sources its produce from local market gardens.

3 O Cachalote, Porto Moniz

MAP C1 ▪ Praia do Porto Moniz ▪ 291 853 180 ▪ Lunch only ▪ €€

Overlooking the natural rock pools, this lively restaurant is popular with tour groups. The menu features regional specialities and fresh, delicious seafood.

4 Orca, Porto Moniz

MAP C1 ▪ Rotunda das Piscinas ▪ 291 850 000 ▪ €

There's a selection of well-presented cheese boards and tapas, plus an eclectic wine list at this café-shop, which also sells souvenirs.

5 Solar dos Prazeres, Prazeres

MAP B3 ▪ Lombo da Rocha ▪ 291 822 759 ▪ €€

Enjoy splendid ocean and mountain views while savouring grilled cod and *espetada de carne* (grilled meat kebab) at this extremely popular eatery.

6 Quebramar

MAP E2 ▪ Sítio do Calhau, São Vicente ▪ 291 842 338 ▪ Closed Mon dinner ▪ €

Tuna steaks and tender medallions of pork are just two of the dishes enlightening the menu at this bright and breezy seafront eatery.

7 O Manjerico, Arco da Calheta

MAP B3 ▪ Caminho da Referta, Pico Prazeres ▪ 965 012 904 ▪ €€

Renowned for its stuffed chicken, this homely eatery is a little off the beaten track but worth the diversion. Call ahead to book.

8 Cantinho da Madalena

MAP C4 ▪ Avenida 1 de Fevereiro 2, Madalena do Mar ▪ 291 624 621 ▪ €€

Grab a seat on the terrace and enjoy a typical Madeiran meal at this local favourite.

9 Borda D´Água, Ribeira Brava

MAP D5 ▪ Rua Engenheiro Pereira Ribeiro ▪ 291 957 697 ▪ €€

Wholesome fresh fish and seafood characterizes the menu at this popular oceanfront venue. Vegetarian options are available.

10 Casa de Chá "O Flo", Ponta do Pargo

MAP A2 ▪ Ponta do Pargo ▪ 291 882 525 ▪ Closed mid-Nov–mid-Dec ▪ €

A teahouse isn't what you'd expect to find on a clifftop, but many come here for homemade soups and light meals.

Casa de Chá

🔟 Eastern Madeira

Most visitors catch a glimpse of Eastern Madeira as they fly in over Machico, the island's second biggest town, and travel from the airport to Funchal along the south coast highway. However, there are wide expanses where no roads go. These include the north coast, with its paths and vertigo-inducing cliffs, and the historic whaling village of Caniçal, the charming town of Santa Cruz and the pastoral landscape of the Santo da Serra plateau, source of the island's wicker.

Steep cliffs of Ponta São Lourenço

① Ponta de São Lourenço
MAP M4

The long, narrow chain of eroded volcanic cliffs and ravines at the eastern tip of Madeira is an exciting and dramatic wilderness, protected as a nature reserve because of its coastal plants. The rocky peninsula can be explored by the much-used path that starts from the car park at the end of the south coast road.

EASTERN MADEIRA

| ① Top 10 Sights | see pp95–7 |
| ① Places to Eat | see p99 |

Ilhas Desertas

Previous pages Traditional A-frame house, Santana district

2 The Ilhas Desertas
MAP J1

Ponta de São Lourenço is linked underwater to the offshore Ilhas Desertas (meaning "Deserted Islands"), which are part of the same volcanic formation. Though arid and uninhabited, these islands nevertheless host all sorts of rare and endangered wildlife, including spiders, monk seals, petrels and shearwaters. For a closer look, contact one of the boat companies *(see p57)* based at Funchal marina, many of which offer day-long trips to the islands.

3 Santa Cruz
MAP K5 ▪ SAM bus 20, 23, 53, 60, 78, 113,156

A town of great character, Santa Cruz is surprisingly peaceful, considering that the airport runway is situated right next door. The focal points are the beach and the seafront, which is lined with cafés and *pastelarias* (pastry shops), as well as the Art Deco-style Palmeiras Beach Lido, painted azure and cream. Set back from the coast, past winding alleys, stands a 15th-century Gothic church, which is as splendid as the cathedral in Funchal, and perhaps designed by the same architect *(see p12)*.

Fortress on the seafront at Machico

4 Machico
MAP K4 ▪ SAM bus 20, 23, 53, 78, 113,156

This is where Captain Zarco and his crew landed on Madeira in 1420. The chapel they founded *(see p47)* is on the eastern side of the harbour. A statue of Machico's first governor, Tristão Vaz Teixeira, stands in front of the main square's 15th-century church. Cobbled alleys lead from here to the seafront. The Solar do Ribeirinho Museum, in a 17th-century manor house, is worth a visit.

Sunbathing on the beach in the pleasant town of Santa Cruz

5 Garajau
MAP J6

A miniature version of Rio de Janeiro's statue of Christ the Redeemer was erected on the wild and rocky headland at the southern end of the village in 1927. The terns (*garajau* in Portuguese) that gave their name to the village can still be seen from the zigzag path that winds down the cliff face to a pebble beach below the headland. Underwater caves and reefs rich in marine life extend for 2 km (1 mile) to either side, and form a marine reserve (*see p98*).

Statue of Christ the Redeemer, Garajau

6 Portela
MAP J4 ▪ SAM bus 20, 53, 78

The viewing point at Portela has more than its fair share of roadside cafés because it was once the transport hub for the east of the island. Tunnels linking São Roque do Faial with Machico have changed all that, but Portela is still an important landmark for walkers. You can walk south from here to Porto da Cruz (*see p84*) along a trail once used by wine carriers, or west along the Levada da Portela through dense primeval woodland and mountain scenery to Ribeiro Frio (*see p83*).

Porto da Cruz seen from Portela

7 Santo António da Serra
MAP J4 ▪ Carros de São Gonçalo bus 77; SAM bus 20, 25, 78

The village of Santo António da Serra (known to Madeirans simply as Santo da Serra), sits in the middle of a plateau flat enough for golf courses (*see p57*) and fields of grazing cows. Despite its frequent cloud cover, wealthy English merchants once built rural homes here: one of the former homes of the Blandy family (*see p17*) is now a public park with camellias, hydrangeas, rhododendrons, deer and horse enclosures, and viewing points that look out toward Ponta de São Lourenço.

8 Caniço de Baixo
MAP J6 ▪ Galomar Lido: open summer 9am–7pm, winter 10am–5pm; adm

Before heading to this charming clifftop holiday village, stop to admire fine Baroque decoration at Caniço's 18th-century Igreja Matriz in Rua João Paulo II. The tiny Praia da Canavieira public beach is reached down an easily missed alley near the junction with Rua da Falésia. For a small sum, you can also use the Galomar Lido. The lido is the base for the Manta Diving Centre, which organizes trips to the Garajau Marine Reserve.

9 Caniçal
MAP L4 • SAM bus 113

A former whaling port, Caniçal is where director John Huston came to shoot the opening scenes of *Moby Dick* in 1956. Unfortunately, its star Gregory Peck became seasick and they had to shoot the rest of the movie in a studio. The Museu da Baleia *(see p49)* uses 3D and interactive displays to explain how conservation has replaced whaling.

Wickerwork demonstration, Camacha

10 Camacha
MAP J5 • Carros de São Gonçalo bus 77, 110, 129; Horários do Funchal bus 113

A monument in the centre of Camacha declares that Portugal's first ever game of football was played here in 1875. The town is famous for its wicker basket industry, and you can still see demonstrations of this traditional craft held on the streets. There are also a few walking trails that pass through here including the Levada dos Tornos and the Levada do Caniço.

THE ILHAS SELVAGENS

Also part of the Madeiran archipelago are the arid, treeless Ilhas Selvagens ("Wild Islands"), which lie 285 km (178 miles) south of Madeira and 165 km (103 miles) north of Tenerife, in the Canaries. These volcanic islets, claimed by Portugal in 1458, have Europe's largest nesting colonies of rare storm petrels and shearwaters. Military sentries from the Nature Guards are stationed on the islands to protect the birds.

A DAY IN EASTERN MADEIRA

🖥 **MORNING**

After breakfast in Funchal, take the south coast highway by following signs to the airport, then take the São Gonçalo exit and head for **Camacha**. The steep road twists and turns before reaching Camacha, which is famous for its wicker – keep an eye out for street demonstrations of the craft. Carry on to **Santo António da Serra** for a walk in the wooded park. Then continue through the village and turn left where the road forks for **Machico** *(see p95)*, known for the Capela dos Milagres *(see p47)* and sandy Banda d'Além beach *(see p52)*. After exploring the town, head for lunch at **Maré Alta** *(see p99)*.

AFTERNOON

The onward drive to **Caniçal** is rewarded with an excellent visitor attraction, the **Museu da Baleia** *(see p49)*. If it's hot and sunny there's also the attractive beach at nearby **Prainha** *(see p52)* to relax on. A little further on is Baía D'Abra, the starting point for one of the most exhilarating coastal hikes in Madeira – the **Ponta de São Lourenço** trail *(see p54)*. Depending on your schedule, you can elect to walk the entire route to Morro do Furado and back, an 8-km (5-mile) ramble of around four hours' duration. Alternatively, try the shorter path to Seahorse Rocks for picture-postcard views and return within the hour. Head back toward Funchal and leave the south coast highway at **Santa Cruz** *(see p95)* for refreshments.

See map on p94 ←

Garajau Marine Reserve Sights

Male Mediterranean monk seal

mammals are seen all over the reserve. Social and playful, they are best observed as part of an organized ocean excursion *(see p57)*.

6 Atlantic Manta Ray

Diving face to face with these majestic fish as they glide gracefully is a real treat. Effortlessly fanning the water, their triangular pectoral fins can span up to 7 m (23 ft) in width.

1 Mediterranean Monk Seal

One of Europe's most endangered mammals, the monk seal is an increasingly frequent visitor to the reserve. Slender, agile and shy, they are more likely to be seen on day trips to the Ilhas Desertas *(see p95)* where a colony of around 30 thrive.

2 Dusky Grouper

The rocky seabed is an ideal habitat for these large, friendly fish. Naturally curious, they'll often swim just an arm's length away from divers.

3 Sperm Whale

A permanent resident of the waters around Madeira, this is the whale species you are most likely to encounter on whale-watching trips *(see p58)*. The best time to see them is from March to September.

4 Trumpetfish

Often seen swimming upright, blending in with vertical coral, these pencil-like fish vary from brown to greenish or yellow. They are very well camouflaged and hard to spot.

5 Bottlenose Dolphin

Year-round residents but here in greater numbers from March to October, pods of these intelligent

7 Loggerhead Turtle

With its slow, deliberate paddle, this gentle and endearing creature always appears as if it hasn't a care in the world. Often seen near the water's surface, loggerheads are considered an endangered species and the reserve provides a welcome sanctuary.

8 Mediterranean Parrotfish

This eccentrically coloured fish can brighten up even the dullest day. Distinguished by its vivid scarlet patch coat replete with yellow trim and silver-blue bands, it is a wonderfully photogenic species.

9 Zino's Petrel

Endemic to Madeira, this is one of the most endangered seabirds of Europe. Elegant in flight, it is seen out at sea during the day; it comes inshore only at night to nest in the high mountainous interior.

10 Great Shearwater

One of six species of shearwater that can be observed off the Madeiran coast, the great shearwater is sighted occasionally in the strait between the island and the Ilhas Desertas, gliding just above the waves, scarcely moving its wings.

→ *See map on p94*

Places to Eat

1 Abrigo do Pastor, Camacha

MAP J5 ▪ Estrada das Carreiras 209 ▪ 291 922 060 ▪ €€

Enjoy hearty, homemade country fare at this rustic eatery (see p61). Leave room for afters, with pumpkin cheesecake a favourite dessert.

2 Muralha's Bar, Caniçal

MAP L4 ▪ Rua da Pedra d'Eira ▪ 291 961 468 ▪ €

The simple vibe here belies some truly delicious food. Try a plate of lapas (grilled limpets drizzled with lemon juice) and a cold beer. Not far from the Museu da Baleia (see p49).

3 Atlantis, Caniço de Baixo

MAP J6 ▪ Ponta D'Oliveira ▪ 291 930 930 ▪ €€

The restaurant appears hewn out of the cliff, and you dine to the sound of the ocean thundering onto the beach. The seafood excels, as do the views.

4 Frente ao Sol, Caniçal

MAP L4 ▪ Sítio da Cerca ▪ 291 961 935 ▪ €€

Delicious grilled fish and seafood, especially the octopus, distinguishes the menu at this friendly eatery.

5 Avó Micas, Santo da Serra

MAP J4 ▪ Porto Bay Serra Golf Hotel, Sítio dos Casais Próximos ▪ 291 550 500 ▪ Dinner only ▪ €€

Tasty Madeiran dishes, including pork marinated in wine and garlic, are served at this homely eatery. Reservations essential.

6 Bar Amarelo, Caniçal

MAP L4 ▪ Caniçal ▪ 291 961 798 ▪ €€

This harbourside gem has a decor of limestone and steel that stands out. Choose from salads, pasta or grilled fish.

PRICE CATEGORIES

For a three course meal for one with half a bottle of wine (or equivalent meal), taxes and extra charges.

€ under €25 €€ €25–€60 €€€ over €60

---

7 Mercado Velho, Machico

MAP K4 ▪ Rua do Mercado ▪ 291 961 129 ▪ €

Set in the courtyard of an old seafront market, this alfresco restaurant serves grilled fish and meat.

8 O Cesto, Camacha

MAP J5 ▪ Rua Maria Ascensão 93 ▪ 291 922 068 ▪ Closed dinner & Thu ▪ €€

Sample traditional Madeiran dishes paired with a poncha (see p65) at this family-run tavern. Specialities include meat stews and the Sopa de Trigo (wheat soup with vegetables, pork and chorizo).

9 Maré Alta, Machico

MAP K4 ▪ Largo da Praça ▪ 291 607 126 ▪ €

The windows afford broad harbour views, and the food is of the ocean, super fresh and served promptly. If there's a table, opt for the terrace.

10 La Perla, Caniço de Baixo

MAP J6 ▪ Quinta Splendida Hotel, Estrada da Ponta Oliveira 11 ▪ 291 930 400 ▪ Open Wed–Sun dinner only ▪ €€€

Seafood risotto au champagne and veal with rosemary exemplify the international menu at La Perla (see p60).

La Perla at Caniço de Baixo

🔟 Porto Santo

Porto Santo lies 43 km (27 miles) northeast of Madeira. Zarco and his crew stopped here in 1418 on their way to explore Africa's west coast. Realizing that the island would be a good base, he returned in 1419 to plant the Portuguese flag here and on Madeira, which was colonized the following year. Early settlers introduced rabbits and goats, which quickly stripped the island of its vegetation, so Porto Santo is not green like Madeira. Instead, the "Golden Island" has a magnificent sandy beach and attracts holidaymakers with its sunshine, sea and agreeable sense of being a very long way from the busy world.

Beautiful golden sands of Porto Santo's wide beach

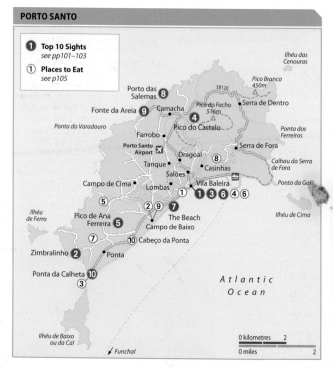

PORTO SANTO

1 Top 10 Sights
see pp101–103

1 Places to Eat
see p105

Ilhéu das Cenouras

Pico Branco 450m

ER120 Serra de Dentro

Porto das Salemas **8**

Fonte da Areia **9** • Camacha

Pico do Facho 516m

Pico do Castelo **4**

Ponta do Varadouro

Farrobo

Ponta dos Ferreiros

Porto Santo Airport

Dragoal

Serra de Fora

Calhau da Serra de Fora

Tanque • Salões

Casinhas **8**

Campo de Cima • Lombas

Vila Baleira **1 3 6** **4 6**

Ponta da Gal

Ilhéu de Ferro

5

2 9

The Beach

Ilhéu de Cima

Pico de Ana Ferreira **5**

Campo de Baixo

7

10 Cabeço da Ponta

Zimbralinho **2**

Ponta

Atlantic Ocean

Ponta da Calheta **10**

3

Ilhéu de Baixo ou da Cal

↙ Funchal

0 kilometres 2

0 miles 2

1 Vila Baleira
MAP L2

All life on the island centres on this city, which sits roughly halfway along the southern coast. Pavement cafés fill the main square, Largo do Pelourinho ("Pillory Square"), where offenders were once punished and public proclamations read out. The town hall, with its double staircase flanked by dragon trees, stands on the site of the pillory. The cobbled pavement in front has a glass-topped, stone-lined pit, which was once used for storing grain.

Nossa Senhora da Piedade

2 Zimbralinho
MAP K2

Boasting transparent blue seas popular with swimmers and divers, Zimbralinho is the most beautiful of all the little rocky coves nestling along the western flank of the island. The cove is at its best around lunch-time, as it is shaded earlier and later in the day. The path to the cove starts at the end of the road that leads to the Centro Hípico (see p104), at the western end of the island.

3 Nossa Senhora da Piedade
MAP L2

To the east of the main square in Vila Baleira stands the majestic parish church, Nossa Senhora da Piedade, completed in 1446. Gothic rib-vaulting and rainwater spouts carved with human and animal heads have

survived from this earlier church, which was torched by pirates, then rebuilt in 1667. The 17th-century altar painting of Christ being laid in his tomb is by Portuguese artist Martim Conrado. The saints on either side were painted in 1945 by German artist Max Römer (see p16).

4 Pico do Castelo
MAP L1

East of Vila Baleira is Castle Peak, though – despite its name – it was never actually fortified. From the 15th century on, it was used as a place of refuge whenever pirates threatened to attack. It was equipped with a cannon, which survives at the lookout point near the summit. A cobbled road leads to the lookout, past the cypress, cedar and pine trees planted to turn the slopes from sandy to green.

Green slopes of Pico do Castelo

Organ pipe rock columns at Pico de Ana Ferreira

5 Pico de Ana Ferreira
MAP K2

Porto Santo consists of a saddle of land between two groups of cone-shaped volcanic peaks. At 283 m (929 ft), Pico de Ana Ferreira is the highest of the summits at the more developed western end of the island. A road up its southern slopes will take you as far as the 17th-century Church of São Pedro. From there, a track leads around the peak to a disused quarry with an interesting formation of prismatic basalt columns known as the "Organ Pipes".

6 Casa Museu Cristóvão Colombo
MAP L2 ▪ Travessa da Sacristia 2–4 ▪ 291 983 405 ▪ Open 10am–12:30pm & 2–5:30pm Mon & Wed–Sat (to 7pm Jul, Aug & Sep), 10am–1pm Sun ▪ Adm ▪ www.museucolombo-portosanto.com/home.html

Christopher Columbus (1451–1506) came to Madeira in 1478 as the agent for a Lisbon sugar merchant.

He married Filipa Moniz, daughter of the governor of Porto Santo, but she died soon after their son was born in 1479 and Columbus left the islands in 1480. The house where they are said to have lived is now a museum, with portraits of Columbus, maps of his voyages and models of his ships.

7 The Beach
MAP L2

Millions of years ago, sandstone, limestone and coral were laid down on top of Porto Santo's volcanic rocks beneath a warm, shallow sea. Falling sea levels exposed the coral to erosion, and the result is the 10-km (6-mile) sweep of sand that runs along the southern side of the island. Backed by dunes and tamarisk trees, the sand is divided into several areas, of which Fontinha and Ribeiro Salgado have been awarded Blue Flag status for environmental quality. Burying yourself in the sand is said to bring relief from rheumatism and arthritis.

Christopher Columbus's house

8 Porto das Salemas
MAP L1 ▪ Camacha
▪ Open daily

This hidden gem is located on the north coast of the island, near Camacha. A steep path leads visitors down to an idyllic coastal spot which features numerous natural pools filled with crystal-clear water. This area is fairly popular for swimming among locals but it still remains a bit of a secret for many visitors. The area is only accessible by foot and the path is unpaved – so be careful not to wear slippery foot-wear. It is best to visit during low tide as this is when you can safely swim in the pools.

 9 ## Fonte da Areia
MAP L1

Water once bubbled straight out of the sandstone cliffs at Fonte da Areia ("Fountain of Sand"), but in 1843 the spring was tamed, and visitors can now taste the natural, rock-filtered mineral water by turning a tap. The path to the spring leads down a wind-eroded gully, where the cliffs have been sculpted into laminated sheets of harder and softer rock.

WATER, WINE AND LIME

Water, wine and lime were once Porto Santo's economic staples. Mineral water was bottled opposite the Torre Praia Hotel access road. Quicklime (used in mortar) made in lime kilns like the one at the Torre Praia was exported. You can still buy Listrão Branco, the local fortified wine, but less is made every year.

 10 ## Ponta da Calheta
MAP K2

The westernmost tip of the island is a beautiful spot, with a series of secluded sandy coves reached by scrambling over rocks. From the bar and restaurant at the end of the coast road, you can look across to Ilhéu de Baixo, the large, uninhabited rocky islet southwest of Porto Santo. Madeira, too, is visible on the distant horizon, usually capped by clouds.

Rocky shore at Ponta da Calheta

A DAY ON PORTO SANTO

▶ MORNING

Hire a car or scooter *(see p104)* for this tour, though you could do it by taxi. Drive northeast out of **Vila Baleira** *(see p101)*, up to the viewing point at **Portela** *(see p96)*. You will see three windmills of a type once common here. Carry on around the eastern end of the island, until a turning to the right takes you down to Serra de Fora beach. Some 2 km (1 mile) fur-ther north are traditional stone houses at Serra de Dentro and fine views from Pico Branco. From the Camacha crossroads, a drivable track to the left leads up **Pico do Castelo** *(see p101)*, soon turning into a stone-paved road. The viewing point at the top has great views over central Porto Santo. Back at Camacha, there are several cafés for lunch.

AFTERNOON

First stop after lunch is **Porto das Salemas** with its pristine natural pools. Then head to **Fonte da Areia**. Despite looking arid, Porto Santo has several natural springs like this one. Alongside the airport runway, you will see some of the vine-yards that still produce wine. Take the road up **Pico de Ana Ferreira**, then continue on foot to see its extraordinary-looking basalt columns. Afterwards, drive on to the stunning western tip of Porto Santo, **Ponta da Calheta**. You should have plenty of time for a drink at **Sunset Bar** *(see p105)*, or a swim before you head back to Vila Baleira.

See map on p100 ←

Activities and Sports

1 Sightseeing
MAP L2

Two-hour tours in open-topped buses depart daily at 2pm from the bus stop by the petrol station on the eastern side of the jetty.

Porto Santo sightseeing bus

2 Exploring by Car
Moinho Rent-a-Car: MAP L2; 291 982 141

Taxis offer island tours, but to explore independently, you can hire a car from Moinho Rent-a-Car.

3 Exploring by Bike
Auto Acessórios Colombo: MAP L2; 291 984 438; www.auto acessorioscolombo.com ▪ Porto Santo Line: MAP L2; 291 210 300

Auto Acessórios Colombo (opposite the road to the Torre Praia Hotel) rents out bicycles, scooters and quad bikes. Bikes can be hired in advance from Porto Santo Line. Collect a bike when you arrive at Porto Santo quay, and return it before the voyage back.

4 Walking
MAP M1

The trail that leads to the top of Pico Branco, Porto Santo's second-highest peak, offers fine views across the island from the Terra Chã lookout.

5 Watersports
Mar Dourado: MAP L2; 963 970 789

Mar Dourado, at Praia da Fontinha beach below the Torre Praia Hotel, rents out pedalos and kayaks, and will organize paragliding, water skiing, windsurfing and boat trips.

6 Tennis
Porto Santo Tennis Academy: MAP L2; Campo de Baixo; 291 983 274

The Porto Santo Tennis Academy is equipped to competition standard. The main stadium has six courts.

7 Diving
Porto Santo Sub: MAP L2; 916 033 997; www.porto santosub.com ▪ Rhea Dive: MAP L2; Hotel Pestana Colombos; 939 333 777

Thanks to the unpolluted seas and the absence of commercial fishing, Porto Santo's shores are rich in marine life. Try Porto Santo Sub or Rhea Dive for diving trips.

8 Horse Riding
Hipicenter: MAP K2; Sítio da Ponta; 291 983 258

Porto Santo's Hipicenter (equestrian centre) will take both children and adults at all skill levels.

9 Shopping
Centro do Artesanato: MAP L2; next to the quay

Shells, model ships and other souvenirs with a nautical theme are the stock-in-trade of Porto Santo's craft shops, which you will find located in the Centro do Artesanato.

10 Golf
Porto Santo Golfe: MAP L2; Sitio das Marinhas; 291 983 778

Designed by Severiano Ballesteros, Porto Santo Golfe has an 18-hole, par 72 course and a 9-hole, par 3 pitch-and-putt course.

The Porto Santo golf course

Places to Eat

PRICE CATEGORIES
For a three course meal for one with half
a bottle of wine (or equivalent meal),
taxes and extra charges.

€ under €25 €€ €25–€60 €€€ over €60

1 Pé na Água, Vila Baleira
MAP L2 ▪ Sítio das Pedras
Pretas Estrada Nacional 111 ▪ 291
983 303 ▪ Closed Tue ▪ €€

Not quite "foot in water" as the name
suggests, but you are right by the
sand at this boardwalk spot. The
chef cooks a great seafood rice, as
well as grilled fish and beef kebabs.

2 Vila Alencastre, Porto Santo
MAP L2 ▪ Estrada da Calheta, Campo
de Baixo ▪ 291 985 072 ▪ Closed Tue
▪ €€

Filete de peixe-espada com banana
(swordfish fillet with banana) and
arroz de pato (duck rice) are specialities at this rustic eatery.

3 Restaurante O Calhetas, Ponta da Calheta
MAP K2 ▪ Cabeça da Ponta ▪ 291
985 322 ▪ €€

Restaurante O Calhetas has an
enviable position at the western end
of the island, overlooking Ponta da
Calheta. Try the seafood spaghetti.

4 Casa do Velho Dragoeiro, Porto Santo
MAP L2 ▪ Rua Gregório Pestana 16a
▪ 291 634 413 ▪ €€

This wonderful hotel-restaurant
serves artfully presented inventive
dishes. The food and wine list are
of excellent value.

5 Restaurante Porto Santo Golfe
MAP L2 ▪ Sítio das Marinhas ▪ 291
983 778 ▪ €€

The vegetarian friendly menu here
mainly features classic Mediterranean
dishes. Tables set on the terrace offer
lovely views over the golf course.

6 Salinas, Vila Baleira
MAP L2 ▪ Rua Goulart
Medeiros (part of the Torre Praia
Hotel) ▪ 291 980 450 ▪ €€

The signature dishes at this stylish
oceanfront eatery include mixed grill
kebab with banana and octopus stew.

7 Adega das Levadas, Miradouro das Flores
MAP K2 ▪ Sítio da Ponta-Morenos
▪ 291 982 557 ▪ Closed mid-Dec–
1 Jan ▪ €

This family-run place is known for its
traditional food, much of it prepared
using home-grown ingredients.

8 Panorama Restaurant & Lounge Bar, Casinhas
MAP L2 ▪ Estrada Carlos Pestana
Vasconcelos ▪ 966 789 680 ▪ Dinner
only; closed Mon ▪ €€

Seriously romantic views make
dining here a special occasion.

Panorama Restaurant and its views

9 Casa d'Avó, Campo de Baixo
MAP L2 ▪ Estrada da Calheta ▪ 291
982 037 ▪ Dinner only; closed Sun,
mid-Dec–mid-Jan ▪ €€

The homely ambience here ensures
a relaxed and fun night out. The local
wines are especially recommended.

10 Bar João do Cabeço
MAP L2 ▪ Sitio do Cabeço da
Ponta ▪ 291 982 137 ▪ €

On the main ER111 road, this friendly,
low-key café-restaurant is a popular
local haunt, especially for lunch.

See map on p100

Streetsmart

**Taxis lining a busy street in
Funchal, Madeira**

Getting Around

Arriving by Air

Madeira's main airport is **Madeira Airport** (also known as Cristiano Ronaldo International Airport), 20 km (12 miles) from central Funchal. It's served by taxis, Madeira airport aerobus and national and international car rental companies. **Tap Air Portugal** flies direct from Lisbon and Porto daily, and connects the island to major European hubs. **Azores Airlines** (SATA) operates scheduled flights between Funchal and Lisbon and Porto. **British Airways** has direct flights from selected UK airports, as do low-cost carriers **Jet2**, **EasyJet** and **TUI Airways**.

There are no direct connections from the US or Canada; instead, flights are routed through Lisbon, Porto or the Azores. Online travel agents, such as **Expedia**, are the fastest way to check flights and prices, as well as hotel and car-hire options.

Porto Santo Airport, in the centre of the island, is not served by public transport: the only way to get there from your hotel is by taxi. Taxis wait at the terminal when flights are due. Alternatively, arrange a pick-up in advance with a specialist airport transfer company. The **Visit Porto Santo** website features a link to tourist taxi service providers.

Arriving by Sea

During July, August and September, **ENM Ferries** operates a car and passenger ferry service between Madeira and Portimão in the Algarve on Portugal's mainland. The island features on a number of cruise itineraries, but passengers usually spend only a few hours in port.

Buses

Buses are an economical and easy way of getting around the island, though services are geared to the peak commuter hours of 8–10am and 4–7pm. **Horários do Funchal** operates all urban services in the city, including wheelchair-friendly Linha Eco minibuses. It also serves selected (inter-urban) destinations in central Madeira including Santana (via Ribeiro Frio), Curral das Freiras and Camacha. For destinations further to the east, including Caniço, Santa Cruz and Machico, look for buses run by **SAM**, which also operates the Aerobus concession, or **EACL**, which additionally serves places such as Garajau. **Rodoeste** runs services to places west of Funchal, and to Porto Moniz and São Vicente on the north coast.

There is no central bus station in Funchal. Instead, buses depart from various points on the seafront (Avenida do Mar). Departure points for interurban routes can be found in the Zona Velha and many Rodoeste buses stop in the Hotel Zone (Lido).

Bus tickets can be bought from the driver.

However, Horários do Funchal city buses need a Giro card, purchased from the driver or from machines set along the seafront. It costs 50c and should then be charged with cash for discounted travel. One- and three-day tickets are available.

Driving in Madeira

Hiring a car gives greater flexibility. However, be aware that parking in Funchal is difficult and metered. Underground car parks are the most convenient option.

All international hire companies have airport and city-centre offices. Local car rental companies, such as **Rodavante** and **Auto Jardim**, often quote better deals.

Taxis

Madeira's yellow taxis are ubiquitous and convenient. In Funchal fares are metered. Journeys are unmetered outside the city. Determine the price beforehand, and don't be afraid to haggle. There are set prices for some pre-defined routes and these are displayed on the back of the driver's or front passenger's seat. The pick-up charge is €2.50 (€3 at night and weekends). You may also have to pay for excess baggage (wheelchairs are free of charge). Companies such as **TaxiMadeira** organize private or personalized half- and whole-day tours of the island.

Cyle and Scooter Hire

Conventional bicycle hire options are limited, but visitors can opt for an electric bike for more relaxed touring and hill climbing. These bikes have an average range of about 25 km (16 miles). You can rent one at **E-Bike Madeira**. Mountain biking is also extremely popular: **Freeride Madeira** is a trusted local operator.

Hiring a scooter is a popular alternative for getting around but bear in mind Madeira's steep roads, hairpin bends and unpredictable weather.

Porto Santo by Air

BinterCanárias operates daily flights at regular intervals between Madeira and Porto Santo. Tickets cost around €130 return. Tap Air Portugal operates two flights a week between Lisbon and the island, and also from Porto Santo during summer.

Porto Santo by Sea

Operated by **Porto Santo Line**, modern car ferries with cinema, restaurants and first- and second-class lounges run to Porto Santo. The journey takes two and a half hours.

Ships leave at 8am daily from Funchal. Return departure times depend on the day of the week and the season. Tickets for the ferry can be purchased online.

The Ilhas Desertas by Sea

Many non-scheduled tour services operate to the Ilhas Desertas ("Deserted Islands"). **Madeira Wind Birds** emphasise bird- and whale-watching. The guides on **Ventura** cruises are marine biologists and naturalists. Both tours depart from the marina at Funchal.

DIRECTORY

ARRIVING BY AIR

Azores Airlines
℡ 296 209 720
ⓦ azoresairlines.pt

British Airways
℡ 217 616 144
ⓦ britishairways.com

EasyJet
℡ 211 222 210
ⓦ easyjet.com

Expedia
ⓦ expedia.com

Jet2
℡ 0333 300 0042 (UK)
ⓦ jet2.com

Madeira Airport
℡ 291 520 700
ⓦ aeroportomadeira.pt

Porto Santo Airport
℡ 291 520 700
ⓦ aeroportoporto santo.pt

Tap Air Portugal
℡ 211 234 400
ⓦ flytap.com

TUI Airways
ⓦ tui.co.uk

Visit Porto Santo
ⓦ visitportosanto.pt

ARRIVING BY SEA

ENM Ferries
℡ 291 210 300
ⓦ madeira-ferry.pt

BUSES

EACL
℡ 291 222 558
ⓦ eacl.pt

Horários do Funchal
ⓦ horariosdofunchal.pt

Rodoeste
ⓦ rodoeste.com.pt

SAM
℡ 291 201 151
ⓦ sam.pt

DRIVING IN MADEIRA

Auto Jardim
℡ 291 524 023

Rodavante
℡ 291 742 448
ⓦ rodavante.com

TAXIS

TaxiMadeira
℡ 912 000 625
ⓦ taximadeira.com

CYCLE AND SCOOTER HIRE

E-Bike Madeira
℡ 926 672 808
ⓦ ebikemadeira.com

Freeride Madeira
℡ 925 977 046
ⓦ freeridemadeira.com

PORTO SANTO BY AIR

BinterCanárias
℡ 291 290 129
ⓦ bintercanarias.com

PORTO SANTO BY SEA

Porto Santo Line
℡ 291 210 300
ⓦ portosantoline.pt

THE ILHAS DESERTAS BY SEA

Madeira Wind Birds
℡ 917 777 441
ⓦ madeirawind birds.com

Ventura
℡ 963 691 995
ⓦ venturadomar.com

Practical Information

Passports and Visas

For entry requirements, including visas, consult your nearest Portuguese embassy or check the **Secretary of State for Portuguese Communities**. An autonomous region of Portugal, Madeira is a full member of the European Union (EU) and part of the Schengen Zone. EU nationals and citizens of the UK, US, Canada, Australia and New Zealand do not need visas for stays of up to three months. Those not from the European Economic Area (EEA), EU and Switzerland will need a valid passport to enter. A number of countries, including the **US**, the **UK**, **Canada** and **Australia**, have embassies in Lisbon.

Government Advice

Now more than ever, it is important to consult both your and the Portuguese government's advice before travelling. The **UK Foreign and Common-wealth Office**, the **US State Department,** the **Australian Department of Foreign Affairs and Trade** and the **Secretary of State for Portuguese Communities** offer the latest information on security, health and local regulation.

Customs Information

You can find information on the laws relating to goods and currency taken in or out of Madeira on **Madeira Airport** website.

There is virtually no limit on the amount of alcohol and tobacco you can bring in from EU countries for personal use. It is illegal to export scrimshaw and other items made from whale teeth and bone.

Insurance

We recommend that you take out a comprehensive insurance policy covering theft, loss of belongings, medical care, cancellations and delays, and read the small print carefully. If your plans include sporting activities make sure the policy covers this.

UK citizens are eligible for free emergency medical care in Madeira provided they have a valid **EHIC** (European Health Insurance Card) or **GHIC** (UK Global Health Insurance Card).

Health

Healthcare in Madeira's main towns is good, however, facilities tend to be relatively basic outside of these urban hubs.

Emergency medical care in Madeira is free for all UK, EU and Australian citizens. If you have an EHIC or GHIC, be sure to present this as soon as possible. You may have to pay after treatment and reclaim the money later.

For other visitors, payment of medical expenses is the patient's responsibility. It is therefore important to arrange comprehensive medical insurance before travelling to Madeira.

Walk-in health centres (centros de saúde) provide non-emergency treatment, but foreign visitors are most likely to be directed to an outpatient department at a hospital.

Travel clinic websites such as **NaTHNac** provide useful sources of information. If extended medical treatment is required, be sure to confirm that the hospital or clinic accepts your insurance coverage.

Foreign visitors do not need any vaccinations, although arrivals from countries where yellow fever is prevalent will need proof of inoculation.

Unless stated otherwise, tap water in Madeira is safe to drink.

Smoking, Alcohol and Drugs

Smoking is banned in most enclosed public spaces and is a fineable offence, although some bars still allow it.

It is illegal to drive under the influence of alcohol. All drugs are decriminalized in Madeira, but possession of small quantities is considered a public health issue and results in a warning or small fine.

ID

By law you must carry identification with you at all times. A photocopy of your passport should suffice. If stopped by the police you may be asked to report to a police station with the original document.

Personal Security

Madeira is safe for visitors, with relatively low crime rates across the island. Never leave valuables unattended, however, and avoid leaving personal items in rental cars, even in the boot. The vehicles are easily recognized by would-be thieves.

To make an insurance claim, you will need to make an official police report; go to the **Funchal Police HQ**. Theft or loss of documents, such as a passport, should also be reported to your embassy.

To contact the fire brigade (bombeiros), ambulance (ambulância) or police (polícia), dial the Europe-wide **emergency number**. Most operators speak English.

As a rule, Madeirans are very accepting of all people, regardless of their race, gender or sexuality.

Homosexuality was legalized in 1982 and in 2010, Portugal became the eighth country in the world to recognize same-sex marriage. Madeira has a fairly discreet LGBT+ community: there are no gay bars, however all establishments on the island are LGBT+ friendly.

Women may receive unwanted attention, especially around tourist areas. If you feel threatened, head straight for the nearest police station.

Travellers with Specific Requirements

TAP Air Portugal, Azores Airlines (SATA) and other airlines offer in-flight and ground support to those with mobility issues – request this at the time of booking. **TUR4all** provides travellers with useful information about

specialist transport services, equipment rental, support products and wheelchair repair. **Disabled Holidays** lists hotel properties suitable for guests with limited mobility and also arranges travel insurance for those with specific requirements.

Most buses are accessible, including Linha Eco minibuses. The cable car to Monte (see pp34–5) is also adapted.

Around 2 km (1 mile) of the Queimadas to Pico das Pedras trail is suitable for wheelchair use.

Funchal's Formasa Beach has been adapted into an Audioplage beach – buoys equipped with sensors line the shore, informing visually impaired visitors (who are fitted with sensor bracelet) about the sea depth and distance from the shore. See the **VisitFunchal** website for more details.

DIRECTORY

PASSPORTS AND VISAS

Australia
Avenida da Liberdade 200, Lisbon
🆆 portugal.embassy.gov.au

Canada
Avenida da Liberdade 196-200, Lisbon
🆆 portugal.gc.ca

Secretary of State for Portuguese Communities
🆆 vistos.mne.gov.pt

UK
Rua de São Bernardo 33, Lisbon
📞 21 392 4000
🆆 gov.uk

US
Avenida das Forças Armadas, Lisbon
🆆 pt.usembassy.gov

GOVERNMENT ADVICE

Australian Department of Foreign Affairs and Trade
🆆 dfat.gov.au
🆆 smartraveller.gov.au

UK Foreign and Commonwealth Office
🆆 gov.uk/foreign-travel-advice

US State Department
🆆 travel.state.gov

CUSTOMS INFORMATION

Madeira Airport
🆆 aeroportomadeira.pt

INSURANCE

EHIC
🆆 ec.europa.eu

GHIC
🆆 ghic.org.uk

HEALTH

NaTHNac
🆆 nathnac.net

PERSONAL SECURITY

Emergency Number
📞 112

Funchal Police HQ
Rua da Infância 28
📞 291 208 400

TRAVELLERS WITH SPECIFIC REQUIREMENTS

Disabled Holidays
🆆 disabledholidays.com

TUR4all
🆆 tur4all.pt

Visit Funchal
🆆 visitfunchal.pt

Time Zone

Madeira keeps Greenwich Mean Time (GMT). Clocks move forward an hour during daylight saving time, from the last Sunday in March until the last Sunday in October, when they move back an hour.

Money

Portugal's currency is the euro. Most urban establishments accept major credit and debit cards. Contactless payments are becoming increasingly common in Madeira, but it is always a good idea to carry some cash for smaller items.

Tipping around 10 per cent is normal when dining out or travelling by taxi; hotel porters and house-keeping will expect €1-2 per bag or day.

Electrical Appliances

Portugal uses plugs with two round pins and an electrical mains voltage of 220V/50Hz. US visitors will need a plug adaptor and a converter, while those from other regions may require only a plug adaptor – check ahead. Most hotel bathrooms offer built-in adaptors for electric razors.

Mobile Phones and Wi-Fi

To use your mobile phone here, it will need to be equipped for GSM frequencies 900 and 1800 MHz. Visitors with EU tariffs will be able to use their devices abroad without being affected by roaming charges. This means that you pay the same rates as you would at home.

Non-EU members can purchase a Portuguese SIM card to use local rates. Check with your carrier whether you need to unlock your device to use a different SIM card.

Most hostels, guesthouses and hotels offer free Wi-Fi (guests are given a password). Free internet access is also widespread, including at the airport, in most hotels, and at many bars, cafés and shopping malls.

Postal Services

The Portuguese postal service is called **CTT Correios de Portugal**. *Correios* (post offices) are usually open 8:30am–8pm on weekdays and 9am–1pm on Saturdays. First-class mail is *correio azul*; second-class is *normal*. *Correio azul* should be posted in blue postboxes, and everything else in red postboxes. Funchal's main post office is **Correios Avenida Gonçalves Zarco**.

Weather

Madeira has a mild, subtropical climate, with average temperatures ranging from 17° C (62° F) in February to 23° C (75° F) in September. October to March has the highest rainfall, especially on the northern side of the island. Porto Santo tends to have fine weather all year round.

Opening Hours

Shops are generally open 9am–1pm and 2–6pm Monday–Friday, and 9am–1:30pm Saturday. In the main towns, larger stores often stay open through lunch. Shopping centres and malls in Funchal, such as **Forum Madeira** *(see p77)*, usually open 10am–11pm Monday–Friday and till midnight at weekends and on holidays. In rural areas, expect shops to close at weekends.

Banking hours are usually 8:30am–3pm Monday–Friday. Madeira's museums generally open 10am–12:30pm and 2–6pm daily – though some close on Mondays.

COVID-19 The pandemic continues to affect Madeira. Some museums, tourist attractions and hospitality venues are operating on reduced or temporary opening hours, and require visitors to make advance bookings for a specific date and time. Always check ahead before visiting.

Visitor Information

Funchal's main **Tourist Information Office** is on Avenida Arriaga. The **Visit Madeira** website is a useful source of information, with lists of tourist offices, approved accommodation and suggestions on where to go and what to do. Other useful websites include **Madeira-Web**, the **Madeira Promotion Bureau**, **Visit Funchal** and the **Madeira Island News** blog. Online magazine **Madeira Live** includes a live webcam

stream from Funchal.
The Best of Madeira is
a free guide to restau-
rants, bars and other
attractions and includes
discount vouchers.
Readers can also
download its free app.

Local Customs

A much-loved aspect of
Madeira is the slow pace
of life. This is evident as
a pedestrian, at public
events and when making
social engagements,
so try to stifle any
impatience and readjust
your tempo suitably.

Madeira retains a
strong Catholic identity.
When visiting religious
buildings ensure that you
are dressed modestly,
with your knees and
shoulders covered.

Language

Portuguese is the official
language of Madeira.
English is widely spoken
in most towns and tourist
resorts, but it is less
prevalent in rural areas.

A little knowledge of
the local language goes
a long way, and locals
appreciate visitors' efforts
to speak Portuguese, even
if you can only manage a
few words.

Taxes and Refunds

VAT is usually 23 per cent.
Under certain conditions,
non-EU citizens can claim
a rebate. Either claim the
rebate before you buy
(show your passport to the
shop assistant and com-
plete a form) or present a
customs officer with your
receipts as you leave. Tax
refund company **Global
Blue** has more details.

Accommodation

Christmas and New Year
are peak periods, with
room rates considerably
higher. Easter, Carnaval
(February or March), July
and August are also busy.
June can be surprisingly
quiet, and enjoys near
perfect weather.

In Madeira, location has
a big influence on price.
City-centre hotels are far
less expensive than the
luxurious five-star hotels
located on the Estrada
Monumental in the west
of Funchal. Prices fall the
further you go from the
city centre and the sea.

Rural properties and
country hotels frequently
feature converted agricultural buildings that have
been turned into self-
contained cottages or
villas. **Madeira Rural** lists
around 20 such options.
Estalagens and *pousadas*
(inns) or *quintas* (manor
houses) are hotels with
great historic character,
often set on an estate
with gardens. **Charming
Hotels Madeira** offers
various options. **Madeira
Apartments** lists hotel
and private apartments
in a variety of locations.

Bed and breakfast
options come in the form
of *pensões* or *residenciais*,
which are clean, basic
guesthouses. Budget
travellers can find hostels
in and around Funchal.
Hostel World lists the
most popular options.

The only campsite,
Parque de Campismo do
Porto Moniz, is located in
Ribeira da Janela. There
is additional camping on
Porto Santo in Fontinha,
right by the beach. The
Visit Madeira website
has more details.

DIRECTORY

POSTAL SERVICES

**Correios Avenida
Gonçalves Zarco**
Avenida G Zarco 9, Funchal
📞 291 202 830

**CTT Correios de
Portugal**
🌐 ctt.pt

VISITOR
INFORMATION

The Best of Madeira
🌐 bestguide.pt

**Madeira Island
News**
🌐 madeiraisland
news.com

Madeira Live
🌐 madeira-live.com

**Madeira Promotion
Bureau**
🌐 apmadeira.pt

Madeira-Web
🌐 madeira-web.com

**Tourist Information
Office**
Avenida Arriaga 16
📞 291 211 902
▦ Open 9am–7pm
Mon–Fri, 9am–
3:30pm weekends
and public holidays
🌐 visitmadeira.pt

Visit Funchal
🌐 visitfunchal.pt

Visit Madeira
🌐 visitmadeira.pt

TAXES AND
REFUNDS

Global Blue
🌐 globalblue.com

ACCOMMODATION

**Charming Hotels
Madeira**
🌐 charminghotels
madeira.com

Hostel World
🌐 hostelworld.com

Madeira Apartments
🌐 madeiraapartments.
com

Madeira Rural
🌐 madeirarural.com

Places to Stay

PRICE CATEGORIES
For a standard double room per night (with breakfast if included), taxes and extra charges.

€ under €100   €€ €100–€200   €€€ over €200

Characterful Hotels

Funchal Design Hotel
MAP P1 ■ Rua da Alegria 2, Funchal 9000-040 ■ 291 780 210 ■ www.funchal designhotel.pt ■ €
Featuring 18 rooms, some with kitchenettes, this contemporary boutique hotel is just a short walk from the city centre. There is an on-site restaurant as well.

Casino Park Hotel
MAP Q1 ■ Rua Imperatriz Dona Amélia, Funchal 9004-513 ■ 291 209 100 ■ www.pestana.com ■ €€
Designed by renowned Brazilian architect Oscar Niemeyer, the hotel hosts dinner dances and professional cabaret. Guests can access Casino da Madeira.

Castanheiro Boutique Hotel
MAP P3 ■ Rua do Castanheiro 31, Funchal 9000-081 ■ 291 200 100 ■ www.castanheiro boutiquehotel.com ■ €€
This 81-room hotel boasts five historic buildings spanning 300 years. Antiques and period furniture decorate the interior, but the rooftop infinity pool is truly a modern perk.

Porto Santa Maria
MAP Q5 ■ Avenida do Mar e das Comunidades Madeirenses 50, Funchal 9060-190 ■ 291 206 700 ■ www.portobay.com ■ €€
An adult-only hotel sited on the water's edge just a few minutes' walk from the old town. Guests enjoy exclusive harbour views, and leisure amenities of indoor and outdoor pools, plus a lovely spa.

Quinta da Bela Vista
MAP G6 ■ Caminho do Avista Navios 4, São Martinho, Funchal 9000-129 ■ 291 706 400 ■ www.belavistamadeira. com ■ €€
The "Beautiful View" is of the wild cliffs to the east, but it could describe the lovely gardens of this traditional manor house.

Quinta da Casa Branca
MAP G6 ■ Rua da Casa Branca 7, Funchal 9000-088 ■ 291 700 770 ■ www. quintacasabranca.com ■ €€
While the manor house retains its 19th-century ambience, rooms in the modern wing are cleverly integrated into the gardens, filled with exotic trees.

Quinta das Vistas
MAP H5 ■ Caminho de Santo António 52, Funchal 9000-187 ■ 291 750 007 ■ www.quinta dasvistasmadeira.com ■ €€
As its name suggests, this carefully renovated 1930s-style manor house affords fabulous views over Funchal. The palm-fringed public areas and spruce gardens lend it a pleasant colonial air.

Quinta do Monte
MAP H5 ■ Caminho do Monte 192-194, Monte, Funchal 9050-288 ■ 291 780 100 ■ www.quinta domontemadeira.com ■ €€
A calm oasis, high above Funchal in a lush, walled garden. The manor at the heart of the estate is set with antique furniture and oriental rugs.

Quinta Mirabela
MAP H5 ■ Caminho do Monte 105-107, Funchal 9050-288 ■ 291 780 210 ■ www.quinta-mirabela. com ■ €€
The original building from 1888 has been sensitively refurbished with a contemporary design that melds old with new. The panoramic terrace is the place to enjoy tasty local and international cuisine.

The Vine
MAP P2 ■ Rua das Aranhas 27, Funchal 9000-044 ■ 291 009 000 ■ www. hotelthevine.com ■ €€
With its stylish and inventive interiors, this city-centre property oozes sophistication. The spa menu lists Madeira wine massage among other options. A plunge pool and the UVA restaurant (see p79) crown the roof.

Casa Velha do Palheiro
MAP H5 ■ Rua da Estalagem 28, São Gonçalo, Funchal 9060-415 ■ 291 790 350 ■ www.casa-velha. com ■ €€€
Celebrated for its gardens (see pp32–3) and excellent golf course (see p57),

the 200-year-old Casa Velha also has a noted restaurant (see p85) and a boutique spa.

Les Suites at The Cliff Bay

MAP G6 ■ Estrada Monumental 145, Funchal 9004-532 ■ 291 707 770 ■ www. portobay.com ■ €€€
A five-star property, Les Suites boasts 23 luxury suites across two beautiful 100-year-old manors and a new contemporary wing. The buildings are connected by lush gardens that afford spectacular views of the Atlantic. The hotel also has an infinity pool and an on-site restaurant, Avista (see p79).

Pestana CR7

MAP Q2 ■ Avenida Sá Carneiro-Praça do Mar, Funchal 9000-017 ■ 291 140 480 ■ www.pestana cr7.com ■ €€€
Named for Portuguese footballer Cristiano Ronaldo and his number 7 shirt, an overnight stay here is an experience where all areas offer total digital convenience. There is also a restaurant, an infinity pool and Museu CR7 (see p48).

Resort Hotels

Meliá Madeira Mare

MAP G6 ■ Rua Leichlingen, Funchal 9000-003 ■ 291 724 140 ■ www.melia madeira.com ■ €€
A spectacular lagoon-pool and state-of-the-art spa are at this upscale resort hotel. A unique experience is the Chef In Your Kitchen service – a private dinner prepared in your room.

Pestana Grand

MAP G6 ■ Rua Ponta da Cruz 23, Funchal 9000-103 ■ 291 707 400 ■ www. pestana.com ■ €€
On Ponta da Cruz headland west of Funchal, the Grand boasts an outdoor pool complex, with seawater meandering through beautiful tropical gardens and swaying palms.

Savoy Saccharum

MAP B4 ■ Rua Serra de Água 1, Arco da Calheta 9370-083 ■ 291 820 800 ■ www.savoysignature. com ■ €€
Overlooking Calheta's marina is a trendy retreat designed by Nini Andrade Silva. The island's sugar cane industry is a theme in the Engenho restaurant.

The Cliff Bay

MAP G6 ■ Estrada Monumental 147, Funchal 9004-532 ■ 291 707 700 ■ www.portobay.com ■ €€€
Surrounded by beautiful terraced gardens leading to palm-shaded pools, this fabulous oceanfront property houses the two-Michelin-starred Il Gallo d'Oro restaurant (see p60). Guest wellbeing extends to a luxury spa.

Pestana Porto Santo

MAP L2 ■ Estrada Regional 163, Sitio do Campo de Baixo, Porto Santo 9400-242 ■ 291 144 000 ■ www. pestana.com ■ €€€
This all-inclusive beach resort features one- and two-bedroom suites and poolside villas. Breakfast, lunch, dinner, snacks and national drinks are all included in room rates. There are comprehensive on-site leisure facilities.

Reid's Palace

MAP G6 ■ Estrada Monumental 139, Funchal 9000-098 ■ 291 717 171 ■ www.belmond.com ■ €€€
World-renowned Reid's has the feel of a country manor house, with art-work, antiques, gardens with pools and great views. A spa and the Michelin-starred restaurant, William (see p79), add to the allure.

Savoy Palace

MAP G6 ■ Avenida do Infante 25, Funchal 9004-542 ■ 291 213 000 ■ www. savoysignature.com ■ €€€
This impressive 352-room hotel melds contemporary design with Belle Époque flourishes. Amenities include a luxurious spa, the largest in Portugal, and a stunning top-floor Galáxia restaurant.

B&Bs and Guesthouses

Casa do Velho Dragoeiro

MAP L2 ■ Rua Gregório Pestana 16a, Vila Baleira, Porto Santo 9400-172 ■ 291 634 413 ■ www.casa dovelhodragoeiro.com ■ €
Attractively furnished, this hotel is one of the best budget options on Porto Santo. Guests can retreat behind stone walls and soak in the pool. Be sure to book ahead for August.

Hotel Salgueiro

MAP B1 ■ Rua do Lugar 34, Porto Moniz 9270-095 ■ 291 850 080 ■ www. salgueiroportomoniz. com ■ €
Upgraded from pensão to hotel, the charming Salgueiro offers stunning views and modern rooms and suites.

Residencial Amparo

MAP K4 ▪ Rua da Amargura, Machico 9200-085 ▪ 291 968 120 ▪ www.amparo hotel.com ▪ €

Acclaimed interior designer Nini Andrade Silva decorated this light and airy guesthouse and its 12 rooms. The restaurant serves hearty Madeiran fare.

Vila Teresinha

MAP N1 ▪ Rua das Cruzes 21, Funchal 9000-025 ▪ 291 741 723 ▪ www. vilateresinha.com ▪ €

Friendly, family-run guesthouse, where some of the rooms have private balconies with great views. Teresinha is located near the Museu da Quinta das Cruzes (see pp18-19).

Residencial da Mariazinha

MAP P5 ▪ Rua de Santa Maria 155, Funchal 9000-040 ▪ 291 220 239 ▪ www.residencial mariazinha.com ▪ €€

Situated on Funchal's oldest street, this lovely inn features a twin room, one suite and a two-bed apartment for four adults. Minimum 3-night stay.

Sé Boutique Hotel

MAP P3 ▪ Rua Sabão 53, Funchal 9000-056 ▪ 291 224 444 ▪ www. seboutiquehotel.com ▪ €€

Located in the heart of Funchal, this modern 54-room hotel features three restaurants and a lush tropical garden, which is set within an inner courtyard. The terrace bar affords splendid city-wide views.

Hotels in Central Madeira

Estalagem Eira do Serrado

MAP G4 ▪ Curral das Freiras 9000-421 ▪ 291 710 060 ▪ www.eirado serrado.com ▪ €

This retreat is a great base from which to hike around the surrounding area and affords spectacular views of the Curral das Freiras (see pp36-7) and its encircling mountains.

Solar de Boaventura

MAP G2 ▪ Sítio do Serrão, Boaventura 9240-046 ▪ 291 860 888 ▪ www. solar-boaventura.com ▪ €

Near the *laurissilva* forest (see p29), this hotel has been converted from a classic 18th-century Madeira house. The rooms are large and a restaurant serves local specialities.

Monte Mar Palace

MAP F2 ▪ Sítio do Montado, nr Ponta Delgada 9240-104 ▪ 291 860 030 ▪ www.monte marpalace.com ▪ €€

Set on a secluded bluff on the island's central northern coast, this hotel has fine Atlantic Ocean and mountain views. Amenities include swimming pools, a pitch and putt course as well as a squash course and a steam room.

Quinta da Serra

MAP F5 ▪ Estrada do Chote 4, Jardim da Serra 9325-140 ▪ 291 640 120 ▪ www.hotelquintada serra.com ▪ €€

Set amid leafy grounds, this beautifully renovated farmhouse offers well-maintained rooms with views of the garden or of the distant sea.

Quinta do Estreito

MAP F5 ▪ Rua José Joaquim da Costa, Estreito de Câmara de Lobos 9325-034 ▪ 291 910 530 ▪ www.quinta doestreitomadeira.com ▪ €€

Once the area's main wine estate, the old house now holds the Adega da Quinta (see p85) and Bacchus restaurants. Modern guest quarters are set in landscaped gardens.

Quinta do Furão

MAP H2 ▪ Estrada Quinta do Furão 6, Santana 9230-082 ▪ 291 570 100 ▪ www. quintadofurao.com ▪ €€

Rooms at this traditionally styled but luxuriously modern hotel enjoy views along the rugged north coast. Set on a headland near Santana, the hotel is noted for its excellent restaurant (see p85).

Hotels in Western Madeira

Calheta Glamping Pods

MAP B3 ▪ Caminho dos Serrões 193 ▪ 968 452 016 ▪ €

These stylish glamping pods in Calheta are entirely made of wood and recycled materials. Wake up with ocean views and enjoy a dip in the pool as you return from a hike to Paúl do Mar (see p54).

Estalagem do Vale

MAP E2 ▪ Sítio das Feiteiras de Baixo, São Vicente 9240-206 ▪ 291 840 160 ▪ www.estalagem dovale.com ▪ €

A historical country-style inn in UNESCO-protected *laurissilva* forest (see p29), this gem has its own pool, spa and restaurant. Minimum 2-night stay.

Hotel Encumeada

MAP E4 ▪ Feiteiras-Serra de Água 9350-000 ▪ 291 951 282 ▪ www.hotel encumeada.com ▪ €
With fine mountain views and amid laurel forest, this large chalet-style hotel is close to some of the best *levada* and mountain paths on the island.

Aqua Natura

MAP C1 ▪ Rotunda da Piscina 3, Porto Moniz 9270-156 ▪ 291 640 100 ▪ www.aquanatura madeira.com ▪ €€
Bright blues and lime greens lend the interior of this family-friendly hotel a light and easy character. Sited near the natural rock pools (see p53).

Estalagem Ponta do Sol

MAP D5 ▪ Quinta da Rochinha, Ponta do Sol 9360-529 ▪ 291 970 200 ▪ www.pontadosol.com ▪ €€
Enjoy views of the setting sun from this stylish clifftop hotel. Distinctive bridges and towers link modern guest quarters with the more traditional public areas, including a glass-walled restaurant.

Jardim Atlântico

MAP B3 ▪ Caminho Lombo da Rocha 1, Prazeres 9370-612 ▪ 291 820 220 ▪ www. jardimatlantico.com ▪ €€
The remoteness of this hotel is part of its charm. Guests can explore the surrounding coast and countryside. Apartments, studios, and bungalows are huge, and there is a mini-market on site.

Savoy Calheta Beach

MAP B4 ▪ Vila da Calheta, Calheta 9370-133 ▪ 291 820 300 ▪ www.savoy calhetabeach.com ▪ €€
Set overlooking Calheta's sandy beach (see p52), this hotel has the feel of a Mediterranean resort. The rooms, suites and apartments are set around an inviting outdoor pool, and there are a couple of good eateries on site.

Hotels in Eastern Madeira

Porto Bay Serra Golf

MAP J4 ▪ Sítio dos Casais Próximos, Santo da Serra 9100-255 ▪ 291 550 500 ▪ www.portobay.com ▪ €
A short stroll from Santo da Serra Golf Course (see p57), this charming place offers a covered pool, spa, gym and library. The Avó Micas restaurant (see p99) is definitely worth trying.

White Waters

MAP K4 ▪ Praceta 25 de Abril 34, Machico 9200-084 ▪ 291 969 380 ▪ www.whitewaters-madeira.com ▪ €
Close to the airport, this family-run boutique hotel with modern architecture has ocean-view rooms. Guests can dine at the restaurant or unwind on the terrace. Machico beach (see p52) is nearby.

Albatroz Beach & Yacht Club

MAP K5 ▪ Quinta Dr Américo Durão, Sítio da Terça, Santa Cruz 9100-187 ▪ 291 520 290 ▪ www. albatrozhotel.com ▪ €€
This 15-room boutique hotel combines a preppy maritime look with traditional island motifs. The fresh- and seawater pools

are enticing, the exotic gardens delightful and the restaurant tempting.

Cais da Oliveira

MAP J6 ▪ Caminho Cais da Oliveira, Caniço de Baixo 9125-028 ▪ 291 934 991 ▪ www.rocamarlido resorts.com ▪ €€
Seemingly sculpted from the clifftop, the hotel's rooms and suites are arranged around indoor and outdoor pools, a restaurant and terraces facing a crystal blue ocean.

Four Views Oasis

MAP J5 ▪ Praia dos Reis Magos, Caniço 9125-024 ▪ 291 930 100 ▪ www. fourviewshotels.com ▪ €€
Hugely popular and good value, this waterfront option can arrange all sorts of leisure activity packages. The popular Praia dos Reis Magos (see p53) is on the doorstep.

Galosol

MAP J5 ▪ Ponta da Oliveira, Caniço 9125-031 ▪ 291 930 930 ▪ www. galoresort.com ▪ €€
The emphasis here is on active tourism, with outdoor yoga, jogging and kayaking among other pastimes. There are also two pools, a spa and plenty of opportunities to do nothing at all.

Quinta Splendida

MAP J5 ▪ Estrada Ponta da Oliveira 11, Caniço 9125-001 ▪ 291 930 400 ▪ www.quintasplendida. com ▪ €€
Tucked away in beautiful botanical gardens, this restored 19th-century manor has 141 rooms, 25 spa suites and three restaurants. The spa is one of the largest in Madeira.

General Index

Acknowledgments

Author

Christopher Catling has written more than 50 travel guides, including best-selling DK *Eyewitness* guides to Florence and Venice. When not writing books, he works as an archaeologist and heritage consultant. He is a Fellow of the Society of Antiquaries and the Royal Society of Arts, and a member of the British Guild of Travel Writers. He loves Madeira, and never tires of visiting it to walk and to enjoy the food and warm hospitality of the islanders.

Special thanks for the invaluable assistance of the Madeira Tourist Board in Funchal, the Madeira Promotion Bureau and the Portuguese National Tourist Office in London.

Additional contributor
Paul Bernhardt

Publishing Director Georgina Dee

Publisher Vivien Antwi

Design Director Phil Ormerod

Editorial Ankita Awasthi Tröger, Rachel Fox, Maresa Manera, Scarlett O'Hara, Sands Publishing Solutions, Sally Schafer, Hollie Teague, Rachel Thompson

Cover Design Maxine Pedliham, Vinita Venugopal

Design Tessa Bindloss, Hansa Babra

Picture Research Taiyaba Khatoon, Ellen Root, Rituraj Singh

Cartography Zafar-ul-Islam Khan, James Macdonald, Casper Morris, John Plumer

Madeira base map derived from Madeira Tourist Board, www.visitmadeira.pt

DTP Jason Little

Production Igrain Roberts

Factchecker Marc di Duca

Proofreader Leena Lane

Indexer Hilary Bird

First edition produced by DP Services, a division of DUNCAN PETERSEN PUBLISHING LTD, 31 Ceylon Road, London W14 0PY

Revisions Parnika Bagla, Marta Bescos, Dipika Dasgupta, Sumita Khatwani, Shikha Kulkarni, Vagisha Pushp, Rohit Rojal, Lucy Sara-Kelly, Anuroop Sanwalia, Beverly Smart, Joana Taborda, Priyanka Thakur, Stuti Tiwari, Vaishali Vashisht, Åsa Westerlund, Tanveer Zaidi

Commissioned Photography Kellie Walsh

Picture Credits

The publisher would like to thank the following for their kind permission to reproduce their photographs:
Key: a-above; b-below/bottom; c-centre; f-far; l-left; r-right; t-top

123RF.com: catafratto 4cla; Wiesław Jarek 97cla; Erich Teister 68cla.

Alamy Stock Photo: ACORN 1 49tr; AGF Srl / Lorenzo De Simone 64br; Arco Images GmbH 89bl; Art Collection 2 19br; K J Bennett 37tr; Paul Bernhardt 23tl, 101b; Bildagentur-online / Sunny Celeste 24t; Philip Bird 56bl; Richard Bond 32–3, 38cla; Clearview 45br; clive thompson travel 37crb; Maurice Crooks 11tl; Park Dale 34br; Martin A. Doe 44cl; eye35.pix 4crb; Doug Houghton Eur 27tl, 44b; Stephen Frost 78tl; Hackenberg-Photo-Cologne 18bc; Hemis 39tl, 51cl, 55cl; George Hopkins 30–31; Ian Dagnall Commercial Collection 16br; Iconotec 6cla, 12bl; imageBROKER 10bl, 26bc, 46t; Karol Kozlowski Premium RM Collection 62b, 101tr; David Kilpatrick 91br; kpzfoto 104tc; Ian Littlewood 11clb; LOOK Die Bildagentur der Fotografen GmbH 33br; Vaclav Mach 73tr; Cro Magnon 63tr; mauritius images GmbH 55br; McCanner 45tl; Graham Mulrooney 35cl; Nature Picture Library 98tl; North Wind Picture Archives 42cl; Paulo Oliveira 65tl; Pictures Colour Library 74b; Pixel Prints 104br; Prisma by Dukas Presseagentur GmbH 4cl; Purple Marbles Madeira 48tl; Radius Images 23cr; Peter Scholey 25tr; Paul Shawcross 39crb, 64cla; Ian Smith 32clb; P Tomlins 3tr; Tromp Willem van Urk 24bl; Sebastian Wasek 33tl; David Wingate 67tr; Jan Wlodarczyk 92–3; Zoonar GmbH 16cla.

AWL Images: Mauricio Abreu 87tr; Peter Adams 96b; ImageBROKER 20t.

Beef and Wines: 79br.

Casa Museu Frederico de Freitas, Funchal: 48b.

Dreamstime.com: Albertoloyo 4t; Aldorado10 11b, 49cl, 54b, 82–3, 84tr, 84clb, 87b; Andersastphoto 28tl; Anitasstudio 2tr, 4clb, 34c, 40–41, 59br, 68b; Anphotos 29tc; Arbaes 4cr; Kushnirov Avraham 80tl; Marilyn Barbone 57tr; Marcel Van Den Bos 12–13, 22bl; Alena Brozova 29bl; Marco Canoniero 43tr; Jiri Castka 7tr; Clickos 10crb, 19cl, 72tl, 75cla; Coplandj 102bl; Henner Damke 3tl, 70–71; Dobs65 95b; Dorinmarius 2cla, 8–9; Aleksandra Durdyn 53tr; Dziewul 54tl, 94cla; Morten Ekstroem 102t; Finaldream 77tr, 86ca; Armando Frazão 66–7, 100ca; Elena Frolova 25bl; Darren Howe 83cl; Nigel Hoy 90cl; Ihb 17tl; Wieslaw Jarek 13tl; Bernd Kelichhaus

51tr, 96ca; Anna Lurye 38–9, 52bl, 82cl; Alexander Mychko 61tr; Philip Openshaw 35tl; Petr Pohudka 36cla; Saiko3p 10cla, 11tr, 13br, 50b; Sandra 4b; Denis Shikov 27bl; John Silva 47cr; Merten Snijders 53clb; Rechitan Sorin 26–7; Nikolai Sorokin 58cla; T.w. Van Urk 58br; Zhykharievavlada 65br.

Getty Images: Henri Bureau 43cla; Luis Davilla 63clb; DEA / G. Dagli Orti 42br; Simeone Huber 7br, 52t; Holger Leue 46bc, 69cl; Frank Lukasseck 28b.

Il Gallo d'Oro: 60t, 79ca.

iStockphoto.com: aqualuso 36–7c, 11crb; Thomas Demarczyk 106–7; PleskyRoman 59tl; Juergen Sack 88–9; saiko3p 81b; Sjo 76b.

Museu de Arte Sacra do Funchal: 10clb, 14c, 14bc, 15tl, 15c, 15crb, 15bl.

Panorama Restaurant: 105crb.

Quinta das Cruzes Museum: © MQC File 18cla

Quinta do Furão: 61bl, 85br.

Quinta Splendida Wellness & Botanical Garden: 99br.

Robert Harding Picture Library: Factoria Singular 16–17; Christian Handl 21cr, 21bl; Michael Jenner 50tc; Michael Nolan 81cr; Ellen Rooney 11cra.

Shutterstock: Balate Dorin 1.

SuperStock: age fotostock 69tr; age fotostock / Karol Kozlowski 95tr, 103bl, / Mauro Tandoi 17crb, / Sebastian Wasek 22–3, 66tl; Hemis / Franck Guiziou 36br; imageBROKER 78c, / imageb / Norbert Probst 57clb, /Stefan Kiefer 88clb; Westend61 56tr.

Cover

Front and spine: **Shutterstock:** Balate Dorin.

Back: **Alamy Stock Photo:** eye35 stock crb, Peter Schickert tl; **Shutterstock:** Balate Dorin b, Balate Dorin clb, Pawel Kazmierczak tr.

Pull Out Map Cover

Shutterstock: Balate Dorin.

All other images © Dorling Kindersley

For further information see:
www.dkimages.com

Penguin
Random
House

Printed in China

First Edition 2005

First published in Great Britain by Dorling Kindersley Limited, DK, One Embassy Gardens, 8 Viaduct Gardens, London SW11 7BW, UK

Published in the United States by DK US, 1450 Broadway, Suite 801, New York, NY 10018, USA

Copyright © 2005, 2021 Dorling Kindersley Limited

A Penguin Random House Company

21 22 23 24 10 9 8 7 6 5 4 3 2 1

Reprinted with revisions
2007, 2009, 2011, 2013, 2015, 2018, 2021

All rights reserved.

A CIP catalogue record is available from the British Library.

A catalogue record for this book is available from the Library of Congress.

ISSN 1479-344X
ISBN 978-0-2415-3860-9

*As a guide to abbreviations in visitor information blocks: **Adm** = admission charge.*

MIX
Paper from responsible sources
FSC™ C018179

This book was made with Forest Stewardship Council ™ certified paper – one small step in DK's commitment to a sustainable future. For more information go to www.dk.com/our-green-pledge

Phrase Book

In an Emergency

Help!	Socorro!	soo-koh-roo
Stop!	Pare!	pahr'
Call a doctor!	Chame um médico!	shahm' ooñ meh-dee-koo
Call an ambulance!	Chame uma ambulância!	shahm' oo-muh añ-boo-lañ-see-uh
Call the police!	Chame a polícia!	shahm' uh poo-lee-see-uh
Call the fire brigade!	Chame os bombeiros!	shahm' oosh bom-bay-roosh

Communication Essentials

Yes	Sim	seeñ
No	Não	nowñ
Please	Por favor/ Faz favor	poor fuh-vor fash fuh-vor
Thank you	Obrigado/da	o-bree-gah-doo/duh
Excuse me	Desculpe	dish-koolp'
Hello	Olá	oh-lah
Goodbye	Adeus	a-deh-oosh
Yesterday	Ontem	oñ-tayñ
Today	Hoje	ohj'
Tomorrow	Amanhã	ah-man yañ
Here	Aqui	uh-kee
There	Ali	uh-lee
What?	O quê?	oo keh
Which?	Qual?	kwahl'
When?	Quando?	kwañ-doo
Why?	Porquê?	poor-keh
Where?	Onde?	oñd'

Useful Phrases

How are you?	Como está?	koh-moo shtah
Very well, thank you.	Bem, obrigado/da.	bayñ o-bree gah-doo/duh
Where is/are…?	Onde está/ estão…?	ond' shtah/ shtowñ
How far is it to…?	A que distância fica…?	uh kee dish-tañ-see-uh fee-kuh
Which way to…?	Como se vai para…?	koh-moo seh vy puh-ruh
Do you speak English?	Fala Inglês?	fah-luh eeñ-glehsh
I'm sorry.	Desculpe.	dish-koolp'
Could you speak more slowly please?	Pode falar mais devagar por favor?	pohd' fuh-lar mysh d'-va-gar poor fah-vor

Useful Words

big	grande	grand'
small	pequeno	pe-keh-noo
hot	quente	kent'
cold	frio	free-oo
good	bom	boñ
bad	mau	mah-oo
open	aberto	a-behr-too
closed	fechado	fe-shah-doo
left	esquerda	shkehr-duh
right	direita	dee-ray-tuh
straight on	em frente	ayñ frent'
near	perto	pehr-too
far	longe	loñj'
up	suba	soo-bah
down	desça	deh-shuh
early	cedo	seh-doo
late	tarde	tard'

entrance	entrada	en-trah-duh
exit	saída	sa-ee-duh
toilets	casa de banho	kah-zuh d' ban-yoo
more	mais	mysh
less	menos	meh-noosh

Shopping

How much does this cost?	Quanto custa isto?	kwan-too koosh-tuh eesh-too
I would like …	Queria …	kree-uh
I'm just looking.	Estou só a ver obrigado/a.	shtoh soh uh vehr o-bree-gah-doo/uh
Do you take credit cards?	Aceita cartões de crédito?	uh-say-tuh kar-toinsh de kreh-dee-too?
What time do you open?	A que horas abre?	uh kee oh-rash ah-bre?
What time do you close?	A que horas fecha?	uh kee oh-rash fay-shuh?
this/that one	este/esse	ehst'/ehss'
expensive	caro	kah-roo
cheap	barato	buh-rah-too
size	tamanho	ta-man-yoo
white	branco	brañ-koo
black	preto	preh-too
red	vermelho	ver-mehl-yoo
yellow	amarelo	uh-muh-reh-loo
green	verde	vehrd'
blue	azul	uh-zool'
bakery	padaria	pah-duh-ree-uh
bank	banco	bañ-koo
bookshop	livraria	lee-vruh-ree-uh
cake shop	pastelaria	pash-te-luh-ree-uh
chemist	farmácia	far-mah-see-uh
market	mercado	mehr-kah-doo
newsagent	quiosque	kee-yohsk'
post office	correios	koo-ray-oosh

Sightseeing

cathedral	sé	seh
church	igreja	ee-gray-juh
garden	jardim	jar-deeñ
library	biblioteca	bee-blee-oo-teh-kuh
museum	museu	moo-zeh-oo
tourist information	posto de turismo	posh-too d' too-reesh-moo
bus station	estação de autocarros	shta-sowñ d' oh-too-kah-roosh
railway station	estação de comboios	shta-sowñ d' koñ-boy-oosh

Staying in a Hotel

Do you have a vacant room?	Tem um quarto livre?	tayñ ooñ kwar-too leevr'
room with a bath	um quarto com casa de banho	ooñ kwar-too koñ kah-zuh d' ban-yoo
shower	duche	doosh
single room	quarto individual	kwar-too een-dee-vee-doo-ahl'
double room	quarto de casal	kwar-too d' kuh-zhal'
twin room	quarto com duas camas	kwar-too koñ doo-ash kah-mash
I have a reservation.	Tenho um quarto. reservado.	tayn-yoo ooñ kwar-too re-ser-vah-doo

Eating Out

Have you got a table for …?	Tem uma mesa para … ?	tayñ oo-muh meh-zuh puh-ruh
I'd like to reserve a table.	Quero reservar una mesa.	keh-roo re-zehr-var oo-muh meh-zuh
The bill, please.	A conta por favor/faz favor.	uh kohn-tuh poor fuh-vor/ fash fuh-vor
I am a vegetarian.	Sou vegetariano/a.	Soh ve-je-tuh-ree-ah-noo/uh
the menu	a lista	uh leesh-tuh
wine list	a lista de vinhos	uh leesh-tuh de veen-yoosh
glass	um copo	ooñ koh-poo
bottle	uma garrafa	oo-muh guh-rah-fuh
knife	uma faca	oo-mah fah-kuh
fork	um garfo	ooñ gar-foo
spoon	uma colher	oo-muh kool-yair
plate	um prato	ooñ prah-too
breakfast	pequeno-almoço	pe-keh-noo-ahl-moh-soo
lunch	almoço	ahl-moh-soo
dinner	jantar	jan-tar
starter	entrada	en-trah-duh
main course	prato principal	prah-too prin-see-pahl'
dessert	sobremesa	soh-bre-meh-zuh
rare	mal passado	mahl' puh-sah-doo
medium	médio	meh-dee-oo
well done	bem passado	bayñ puh-sah-doo

Menu Decoder

açorda	uh-sor-duh	bread-based stew
açúcar	uh-soo-kuhr	sugar
água mineral	ah-gwuh mee-ne-rahl'	mineral water
alho	ahl'-yoo	garlic
amêijoas	uh-may-joo-ush	clams
arroz	uh-rohsh	rice
assado	uh-sah-doo	baked
atum	uh-tooñ	tuna
azeitonas	uh-zay-toh-nash	olives
bacalhau	buh-kah-lyow	dried, salted cod
batatas	buh-tah-tash	potatoes
batatas fritas	buh-tah-tash free-tash	french fries
bica	bee-kuh	espresso
bife	beef	steak
bolo	boh-loo	cake
café	kuh-feh	coffee
caranguejo	kuh-rañ gay-yoo	crab
carne	karn'	meat
cebola	se-boh-luh	onion
cerveja	sehr-vay-juh	beer
chá	shah	tea
chouriço	shoh-ree-soo	red, spicy sausage
cogumelos	koo-goo-meh-loosh	mushrooms
cordeiro	kur-deh-roo	lamb
dourada	doh-rah-dah	sea bream
fiambre	fee-ambri	ham
frango	fran-goo	chicken
frito	free-too	fried
fruta	froo-tuh	fruit
gambas	gam-bash	prawns
gelado	je-lah-doo	ice cream

gelo	jeh-loo	ice
grelhado	grel-yah-doo	grilled
leite	layt'	milk
manteiga	mañ-tay-guh	butter
marisco	muh-reesh-koosh	seafood
ostras	osh-trash	oysters
ovos	oh-voosh	eggs
pão	powñ	bread
pastel	pash-tehl'	cake
peixe	paysh'	fish
pimenta	pee-men-tuh	pepper
porco	por-coo	pork
queijo	kay-joo	cheese
sal	sahl'	salt
salada	suh-lah-duh	salad
salsichas	sahl-see-shash	sausages
sopa	soh-puh	soup
sumo	soo-moo	juice
tomate	too-maht'	tomato
vinho branco	veen-yoo brañ-koo	white wine
vinho tinto	veen-yoo teen-too	red wine
vitela	vee-teh-luh	veal

Numbers

0	zero	zeh-roo
1	um	ooñ
2	dois	doysh
3	três	tresh
4	quatro	kwa-troo
5	cinco	seeñ-koo
6	seis	saysh
7	sete	set'
8	oito	oy-too
9	nove	nov'
10	dez	de-esh
11	onze	oñz'
12	doze	doz'
13	treze	trez'
14	catorze	ka-torz'
15	quinze	keeñz'
16	dezasseis	de-zuh-saysh
17	dezassete	de-zuh-set'
18	dezoito	de-zoy-too
19	dezanove	de-zuh-nov'
20	vinte	veent'
21	vinte e um	veen-tee-ooñ
30	trinta	treeñ-tuh
40	quarenta	kwa-ren-tuh
50	cinquenta	seen-kwen-tuh
60	sessenta	se-sen-tuh
70	setenta	se-ten-tuh
80	oitenta	oy-ten-tuh
90	noventa	noo-ven-tuh
100	cem	sayñ
101	cento e um	sen-too-ee-ooñ
200	duzentos	doo-zen-toosh
500	quinhentos	kee-nyen-toosh
1,000	mil	meel'

Time

one minute	um minuto	ooñ ee-noo-too
one hour	uma hora	oo-muh oh-ruh
half an hour	meia-hora	may-uh oh-ruh
Monday	segunda-feira	se-goon-duh-fay-ruh
Tuesday	terça-feira	ter-sa-fay-ruh
Wednesday	quarta-feira	kwar-ta-fay-ruh
Thursday	quinta-feira	keen-ta-fay-ruh
Friday	sexta-feira	say-shta-fay-ruh
Saturday	sábado	sah-ba-too
Sunday	domingo	doo-meeñ-goo

Selected Index of Places